Jerry Baker's Growth Plan For People

The PMA Book Series
W. Clement Stone, General Editor
Robert C. Anderson, Editorial Consultant

This series of books presents practical approaches
to achieving success and fulfillment in business,
professional, and personal life.

Based on the proposition that there is an
intelligent solution to every human problem and
that with a positive mental attitude (PMA) a person
can overcome any adversity, each book in this
series offers practical, step-by-step advice and
inspiration to action.

Titles in this Series Include:

Jerry Baker's Growth Plan For People

Jerry Baker

DODD, MEAD & COMPANY
NEW YORK

Published by Dodd, Mead & Company, Inc.
71 Fifth Avenue, New York, N.Y. 10003
Manufactured in the United States of America

First Edition

1   2   3   4   5   6   7   8   9   10

Library of Congress Cataloging-in-Publication Data

Baker, Jerry
    [Growth plan for people]
    Jerry Baker's growth plan for people / Jerry Baker—1st ed. p. cm.—
    (PMA book series)
    Includes index.
    1. Success. I. Title. II. Series.
    BF637.S8B32 1988
    158′.1—dc19   87-32042
    ISBN 0-396-08972-0   CIP
    ISBN 0-396-08973-9 {PBK}

Contents

Acknowledgments

In all of the books I have written, I find the acknowledgments the most gratifying and yet most difficult. Like an entertainer who has just been named recipient of a major award on national television in front of millions of people, you are expected to give credit to all of the people who helped you to be in the position to receive this award, only the director informs you that you only have three minutes, and your list is the size of the Manhattan phone book.

I am always afraid I will forget someone who helped me when I really needed it.

I wish to acknowledge God and thank Him for all that I am and all I have received. Without His love and understanding, I would be nothing.

To my wife, Ilene, whose life I have made most difficult through my lesson learning days, I love you beyond words.

To my children, Sue, Diane, Patti, Jeff and Kassie, I am so proud of each of you that only my future actions can repay you for any pain I caused you by not being there when you needed me.

To Jim Greene, Ed Karras, Norm Milley, Owen Reinert and Bob Armstrong, I can never repay you for the confidence and support you gave me on my return trip up the mountain. You are the greatest team I have ever had the privilege to play for.

To Alcoholic's Anonymous, Thank God you are here!

Pregame Warm-up

Dr. J. Tyson Tildon wrote in the preface to his book *The Anglo-Saxon Agony**: "It is the maximum audacity that any author should attempt to define a particular sociological posture of man." He went on to write that he hoped his recklessness would be buffered by the fact that his thoughts, suggestions, and statements were not final, but part of a continuing dynamic development of a larger knowledge.

That, my friends, sums up my feelings about writing a book to be used as a guide to attempt to accomplish what may seem impossible.

I know the value of such guidance because I received a lot of it from Dr. Tildon in my own tour to success. His help has been tantamount to having a real live angel looking over my shoulder and guiding me all the way.

That a former narcotic cop, soldier of fortune, gardener, entertainer and writer could possibly know the secrets to success may seem ludicrous. But what you are about to read is based on experiences I've had on my journey to the wonderful world of success. Along the way, I'll point out obstacles that you might avoid or detour around.

Dr. Tildon taught me that all learning requires the awesome transition from a state of not knowing to one of knowing. This book is offered as another bridge for such a crossing.

I am not an old and wise man and I don't have years of higher education. In high school I just barely squeezed by. I am not bragging or complaining, merely stating a fact.

---

*Tildon, J. Tyson. *The Anglo-Saxon Agony*. Philadelphia, PA: Whitmore Publishing Co., 1972.

I have never been president or chairman of the board of any of America's major corporations nor do I have any such goal. Running a big company isn't my thing and just thinking about it would, I am sure, inhibit my personality.

So why should advice from me be of any use to those of you who have graduated from college or may already be presidents, board chairmen or top managers—or at least are on your way to attaining such positions?

To tell the truth, I'm not sure that you will be able to get any use out of it at all, unless you are a goal seeker—unless there is still something you want, are willing to ask for it, and then work like hell to get it and keep it.

No matter who you are or what you are, whatever your race, religion or nationality—man or woman—you can make it. Having advanced education can shave some time off the period required to get results. Education can give you some theory to fall back on in your chosen field while others have to take time out for research. But, it doesn't make you any different, or any better.

If you are a goal seeker, you are a person who doesn't want to be just one of the crowd. You want the fame, fortune, power, and independence that comes with recognition.

You are self-centered, possibly even selfish, keenly sensitive, and aware of all of your strong points as well as weak points, physically, and mentally.

You have one of the best built-in guidance systems ever devised and it's based on the fact that you know who you are, where you are, and where you wish to go. You also like yourself. You are a goal seeker.

You wish that all good things could happen for your family and friends, but realize that they, and they alone, are responsible for their actions and reactions as individual personalities, so you must learn to separate your social activities and attitudes from your goal orientation if you are to be a successful goal seeker.

I am a former Detroit policeman. For a number of years I did all of the things policemen do: pounded a beat, did scout car duty, vice detail, narcotics investigation, and so on. Being a police officer was a childhood ambition and I fulfilled it. I highly recommend that all goal seekers get their childhood ambitions out of the way before they begin in earnest.

However, I can't recall a day I didn't enjoy being a policeman. I loved the challenges of that job. In those years, I learned more about human behavior and my own mental and physical capabilities than I could have learned in seventy years of normal living. It was then I discovered that the secret of success lay in how I conducted myself and influenced others to help me get where I wanted to go. That's when I became a goal seeker.

I learned to shape my conduct to attain my goals. Since then, I have been able to improve on the technique until it's darned near down to a science.

As a police officer, I learned the value of blind faith. I had to have faith in my partner. My life depended on it. When two people work together in life-or-death situations, all prejudice disappears. Nothing counts but the two of you, keeping one another alive.

I can honestly say I never feared for my life, no matter how tight the situations were—and there were many tight ones—because we were there to first keep each other alive, then save the victim, and then apprehend the criminal.

In the business world, the goal seeker quickly discovers one very important thing. There is no one in whom you can put blind faith. There is no one to look out for your back. You are totally alone. I have arrested pimps, con men and thieves who had more morals than some of the people I have dealt with in the business world.

The police ·department, however, could not supply all my wants for recognition and income, so I looked for a vehicle that could offer me the opportunity to gain those goals.

I moonlighted as a salesman. I got a job selling seed and fertilizer to the truck farmers who brought their produce to market each morning. I would work from eight at night to four the next morning as a vice officer, sleep in a cell block for a couple of hours, and get up for the early morning market.

Down at the market, I placed a bright green derby on my head so the produce growers could tell me from the buyers. I got attention, made sales. And I didn't stop there.

My employer had a few products for consumer use, so on my way home I'd make sales calls at retail dealers. It was tough to sell these dealers, because larger distributors with a greater variety of merchandise had more to offer. My employer was an ultraconservative business man who didn't believe in buying merchandise until he, in turn, had a buyer for it. The most he'd allow for back-up merchandise was five percent over firm orders. To sell retailers, I had to change my employer's attitude, get him to agree to carry more variety and reasonable inventories. Then I had to establish recognition and credibility with the dealer. I had to make the dealer believe there was room for yet another wholesale distributor. And, I had to do this while maintaining our established business with growers on the market each morning—following night after night on a grueling police beat!

I began by personally surveying the total consumer garden market at the retail level. I noted the most popular brands and the best-selling numbers and sizes in each line. I listed the volume of every dealer from the largest to the smallest. Most important, I made a list of retail outlets which could have a potential for my merchandise but were not being serviced by my competitors. I discovered three types of locations: variety stores, small groceries, and large chain groceries.

I then went to my employer and reviewed his inventory to see what we could offer this neglected market. I found that we could put together an assortment of small packaged plant foods and accessory products that could fit into the small spaces allocated to plant and garden merchandise in variety and grocery outlets. Next, I began to look for line extensions in products that had national advertising exposure and a good profit structure. I knew that extending the line would tax my employer's capital, but I thought I had found just the baby I wanted.

Standard Oil of California's Ortho garden products looked just like the ticket, but Ortho in those early years refused to let me put their products into grocery stores. Union Carbide, however, had noted Ortho's success in other markets and decided to go into the business itself using one of their own recognized trade names—Eveready. Union Carbide went full tilt into the lawn and garden chemical business with a one-on-one against Ortho. They put out merchandise racks you wouldn't believe—top quality. Well, to make a long story short, I went to Union Carbide and was welcomed with open arms and all the trimmings—delayed billing, bonus, quantity discounts, store door delivery, and guaranteed sale. Grocery stores? "Go get 'em!" they said, and overnight I became the number one garden product salesman in the country. Soon there wasn't a grocery store anywhere without one of my merchandisers in it. I then proceeded to suggest other accessories.

Another company, Dow, popped up with a new crabgrass control. Dow was also offering a lot of fringe benefits to the merchants.

While I was at it, I talked Union Carbide into giving me a franchise to sell Eveready batteries. This helped break the ice with a lot of dealers, especially when I showed them how to sell batteries at the check-out, something they hadn't thought of before. Then, for the garden line, I made up a little catalog. It was thin and didn't even have photographs, just some line drawings in the margin to idenify the goods. The rest of each page was an automatic inventory control system that helped the dealers to determine their sales, inventory on hand, profit and loss at any given time.

I was making friends, but I needed some publicity, so I talked a reporter into doing the usual story on the opening of the garden market in the spring, but with a new twist. The hero of the story would be yours truly, the man with the green derby, "The Pied Piper of the Pickle Patch," the man with the answers to gardening problems—and it worked. Now, I had identity, some recognition, and dealers looked forward to having me come in.

Business boomed and my cover collapsed. I soon left the police department and went into the garden patch full-time, only to find that my employer was getting petrified by all this success and wanted to stop where he was! That was when I learned something else—which is that a lot of people can take failure easier than they can take success. We're so used to just floundering along and never reaching our goals that we panic when we're suddenly faced with a real success! Naturally, that's the one thing most folks don't have much experience with.

But now, along came another new baby, Kresge Company's Kmart. They needed a garden merchandiser and supervisor. After I took the job, it didn't take me long to realize that even though they were mass merchandisers, their garden department was seasonal only. What they needed was to attract some attention. I figured if a green hat on a six-foot, four-inch guy got attention, what would a kelly green suit, vest and overcoat do? It did attract attention. Not only the suit, but my big bright crest that read "Mr. Grow-It-All." I talked a local car dealer into painting up a white van with vines and ivy and the name, "Mr. Grow-It-All," on the sides. I drove the streets and would speak at any club, church, or garden club. I talked at schools and then I began answering garden questions on Bob Allison's *Ask Your Neighbor* show. The *Detroit Free Press* asked me to write a column. Dan Kibbie brought me to TV with the ABC *Morning Show*. Kmart Garden Centers became the place to shop, and you might even meet Mr. Grow-It-All. Enthusiasm among store managers was terrific, but some management resented an outsider gaining such fame and attention. They were sure my motive was self-advancement at their expense which was total foolishness, because my income was based on *their* increased sales.

Mr. Grow-It-All was a name I had dreamed up. The company thought the name should be protected, and it was, but not for me. Then I was told that I had no future beyond my present position because I had not traveled the prescribed route from trainee to management.

This goal seeker now took off his disguise. I had to prove that I was not an opportunist, but an *opportunity*. Now it was time for me to establish my own identity, to get out from under my own monster, Mr. Grow-It-All.

This was when I devised my first real game plan and a goal. Since I was in heavy demand as a speaker with a humorous approach to gardening, I decided to give Ortho folks another chance to help me. I suggested that in exchange for publicity for Ortho they give me an award because of all the interest I was generating in home gardening. First they agreed and then asked, "What type of award?" "How about the 'American Master Gardener Award'?" I asked. Very good—a luncheon and press conference was arranged so Jerry Baker could become America's Master Gardener, complete with a plaque and a telegram from Ortho's president. Mr. Grow-It-All moved toward retirement and Jerry Baker, America's Master Gardener, came into the limelight. This time I did protect my name, and America's Master Gardener became my registered trademark. National TV appearances followed, climaxed with the Dinah Shore *Dinah's Place* show, thanks to my mentor, Dan Kibbie.

It was now becoming impossible to fulfill my obligations to the fast-moving expansion of the Kmarts, maintain my personal appearance schedule, television production schedule, and new book commitments. So I found it necessary to leave yet another job I thoroughly enjoyed. The early years in Kmart were exciting as well as educational. I received a lesson both in theory and practice on how to merchandise in a grand scale.

After moving on from Kmart, I took that lesson and applied it to my personal career. I packaged and merchandised myself in a realistic way the same as I would a bag of lawn food, mower, or potted plant. I displayed my product, priced it, advertised it and sold the dickens out of it. Since *Plants Are Like People*, my first book, I have added several dozen other titles—selling millions of copies, syndicated on television, radio and in hundreds of newspapers. I cut a highly successful record album for MGM called *Plants Are Like People*, released video cassettes for Simon & Schuster, appeared at the Chicago Opera House in a how-to musical comedy on plant care called "An Evening With Jerry Baker and His Plants."

In 1981 I had a discussion with my former boss at Kmart, Norm Milley, who had now become Sales Director, about becoming a company spokesperson. I gladly agreed, since one of my goals was to return to the team that helped me launch my career. Kmart is the only retailer that I know of that uses a talent spokesperson to its maximum potential, in ways that benefit both the talent and the company. The beautiful Jacqueline Smith, fashion designer and spokeswoman for Kmart apparel, and I are directly involved with formulation, design, training, promotions and travel to attain the goals that we help set for the success of both of our areas of expertise. I am directly associated with the Super K-Gro private label brand and the garden departments.

Some people will say it's mostly luck, that it would have happened whether I set goals or not. To a certain extent, that is right. My Grandma Putnam, about whom I write so much in my garden books, told me once that luck was being in the right place at the right time, recognizing the opportunity and then taking advantage of it. She said that constantly "lucky" people always kept their eyes and ears open. Finding an opportunity often *is* luck, but knowing how to *build* an opportunity isn't. And I knew when to build.

If you aren't equipped physically or psychologically to play the game, then just be a spectator. It won't be as exciting or rewarding, but after all, that is how most people live—watching things happen instead of *making* them happen.

If something I say along the way helps you achieve a goal, then I'll know it was worth the time it took to write this book. If you discover the real you, it was worth it. If you discover that every individual is exactly that and has the same right to opportunities you have, it's worth it. If you discover that you can do it without extra help from others, it's worth it. If you can decide you really want it, then it's *really* worth it.

In all sports there are what they call basic fundamentals. You must learn them—and well. From that point on, each coach develops his own style, one in which he feels comfortable. This book is a basic and fundamental guide for the goal seeker. Like the coach, once you master the fundamentals, you should alter things to fit your own style. Remember that at all times.

It's never too late to become a goal seeker. If you are at an impasse in your present job or career, check the exits. If you feel the squeeze is being put on you, you may be in a goal seeker's game and not know it. If you want to control your own destiny, if you don't want to leave it in the hands of others who will, for their own selfish reasons, never let you get ahead of them, then you had better seriously consider trying the goal seeker's way.

Women, even more than men, should practice the goal-seeker strategy, which automatically places a person on the offensive side. On the whole, I have found that women in business are more aware, more sensitive and more creative—not to mention more determined—than men. In the goal-seeking arena, some of my toughest games have been against women, and I have the scars to prove it. On the other hand, some of my best players have been women.

There is no discrimination in the thrilling, self-satisfying and rewarding game of goal seeking. By the same token, no unearned advantage is given for any reason.

As you read on, you will find that from time to time I will be redundant. I intend to be. There are points that I want to drum into your heads until they are second nature (or automatic alerts). Pay attention!

Nobody can promise you overnight success, but you *can* become a goal seeker overnight if you want to. Blue collars, greasy overalls, or gray flannel suits will do for uniforms. Housewives, waitresses, clerks, secretaries, and professional women are welcome to the game. Even lion tamers will find new excitement here. Anybody who wants that little extra out of life can discover how close at hand it is if you're willing to work for it.

Women may find goal seeking a bit difficult to adjust to at first, because they have been told that their place is in the home (cooking, cleaning and raising children) and that the only jobs considered proper for them are as clerks, teachers, beauticians, nurses or waitresses. What a crock! If you have an education or a talent to make a mark in society, then go for it! Housekeeping and child rearing are a joint responsibility of both parents.

Are You Ready?

1. Are you pleased with your present self?

2. Are you pleased with your present lifestyle?

3. Are you pleased with your job?

4. Are you pleased with your present marriage or relationship?

5. Are you pleased with your present group of acquaintances?

6. Are you pleased with your attitude toward religion?

7. Are you pleased with the present day attitudes of society?

8. Are you pleased with your present material worth?

9. Do you have a best friend in whom you would put blind faith?

10. Are you ashamed to admit when you make a mistake publicly?

If you answer two or more of these questions with a "*no*," you are a candidate for the game of goal seeking.

Chapter 1

Ground Rules
About Goals

Goals are something most people never give much thought to. The majority of those I come in contact with are of the belief that what will be, will be, and that nothing they do or don't do will have any bearing on the outcome of health, wealth, happiness, longevity, or success.

There is a great deal more to living than simply existing until death. We owe our creator more than a cursory attempt at success or relying on him to provide us with both our needs and wants.

Success comes only to those who work for it, not wish for it. Success comes through planning and persistence.

The first and most important step is to know what it is you really want to accomplish. This is called a *Goal*. If you plan to take a trip, your final destination is your goal; and in order to get there as quickly and safely as possible, you follow a map, a planned route! This is precisely what you must do in life, if you are to succeed. Set goals and then map out the trip to get there safely and as quickly as possible.

Goals can vary from simple "short trips" to very complicated ones "long range." The only thing necessary to remember is that in setting your goals you should be realistic about both the practicality of your plans and the time necessary to implement them.

Goals should never be a spur-of-the-moment decision. Take your time picking the right goals. Remember you will be spending the rest of your life working them out.

Sincere goal seekers will end up contributing more to society as they journey through life than they ever take out of it. As a goal seeker, you will never be considered a waster of time or a taker-up of space; you will be viewed as a builder and contributor.

When I launched my Mr. Grow-It-All campaign, it was my goal to become the best-known consumer garden adviser in the country, thus increasing my value as a product salesman for my sponsors. This goal had three major objectives, which demanded that I (1) gain consumer exposure, (2) attain credibility, and (3) merchandise my services.

I chose home gardening because it was emerging as a field of booming consumer interest. It also was a vast field with no dominant personality in it, and I had both the interest *and* the knowledge of gardening needed to become that dominant personality.

All that remained was to devise a workable plan to achieve my goal.

Through trial and error, I found a formula for achieving *any* goal. All it required was a willingness to learn—and practice—certain fundamental rules and positive creative exercises. The list starts with a big "Don't."

Don't Get Goals Mixed Up with Wishes, Dreams and Visions

I have met very few persons who are satisfied with either their positions in society or the material objects or savings they have acquired. They do not believe they are being adequately paid for the work they are performing, and they'll inform you that they could do a better job than their immediate superior or any other member of management all the way to the top. When you suggest that they should challenge their immediate superior by informing him that he is incompetent and that they could do the job better, however, they get sheet-white with fear and ask you to forget what they said.

They'll say they were just fooling. You bet they were—fooling themselves.

Folks like these are perfectly secure on their own little Peter-Principle shelves. That is, they have risen to the pinnacle of their own incompetence. They seem to get some kind of perverse pleasure out of thinking they're being exploited by management, but in most cases, if they were offered greater responsibility with additional income based on their performance and results, they would panic. They are literally more afraid of success than failure.

For centuries, man has been dissatisfied with his lot in life and has made dramatic progress in changing it. But the forward strides have been the work of a few goal seekers. Most men just go along with things the way they are. Oh, I know they may complain as they're bellied up to the corner bar—about how they would change this or that in their life or their job—but they still continue along the same old rut year in, year out. Such folks usually don't change a thing—except maybe their underwear.

There are those who look off into space and see themselves sitting in an executive suite or cruising on a yacht in the Caribbean, surrounded by big cars, servants at their fingertips, wine, women (or men) and song. Others of different tastes picture themselves as full professors, professional athletes or in a multitude of other dream positions. For any of these folks, a tap on the shoulder, a phone ringing or some other distraction breaks the vision and dashes it to pieces as quickly as it came.

Both of these types—the griper and visionary—are dreamers who would find it difficult to join the team of goal seekers. To get you started on the right foot and further clarify who falls into the category of the "non-goal seeker," like those types just mentioned, I refer to *Webster's Dictionary* for the definition of *dreamer:*

> **dream·er** one who dreams, one who lives in a world of fancy and imagination, one who has ideas or conscious projects regarded as impractical; visionary.

I suggest that you draw red lines under this definition so you can refer back to it when you begin to set goals. It will be a test of great practical value.

In the Pregame Warm-up section, I told how I decided to draw attention to my garden department in the Kmart stores by dressing up in a completely green wardrobe, giving myself the catchy name

of Mr. Grow-It-All and driving around in a wildly decorated van sup-
plied by a local auto dealer at no cost to my employer. Needless to
say, more than one eyebrow was raised by both my former peers in
the gardening business and Kresge's management—not to mention
the static my immediate superiors caught for allowing me to make
such a spectacle. At the same time, my former competitors were
quite happy to see me making, in their opinion, a fool of myself.

The truth of the matter was that I had *planned* to be laughed at,
especially by those who wouldn't recognize an opportunity if it fell
on them. Indeed, I would have been disappointed if those fellows
had *not* laughed their fool heads off.

My goal was to create recognition through visual association and
I took the necessary steps to make it happen. Note those words,
"*make* it happen." I didn't wish it to happen. I didn't dream it would
happen. I set a goal and *made* it happen.

Don't Play Another Person's Game

You must avoid, at all cost, setting goals for *yourself* based on another person's wants or needs. I have watched husbands and wives
and sons and daughters make a decision to attempt something that
someone else wanted them to do, and then when they failed, the
person putting the pressure on them blamed them for the decision.
This often occurs in credit obligations (new cars, bigger houses,
elaborate vacations) or career decisions or changes (new jobs, college majors). A goal requires that you spend time and effort—ele-
ments of *your* life that are not replaceable and that you can't afford
to waste.

No One Can Pull You into Heaven
nor Push You into Hell

When you make a decision to set a goal, don't try to fool yourself
into thinking that reward is anything but satisfaction. You are totally
responsible for your actions or inactions as well as for the quality
of the goal itself. Never let vengeance become a goal.

Opportunity Knocks More than Once

We have heard the reverse of this slogan since we were old enough to understand the meaning of the word *opportunity*. The only opportunities that are truly fleeting, passing our way only once, are things like marrying the daughter of the boss or finding a million dollars in small unmarked bills on the front seat of our car with a note saying, "Enjoy!" As for the more *realistic* opportunities that come our way, such as the chance for more rapid advancement in a job or career or the potential for recognition, financial independence, better grades or any of hundreds of other desirable ends . . . these possibilities present themselves any time you are prepared to attempt to conquer them. George Bernard Shaw said it best in his play, *Mrs. Warren's Profession:*

> The people who get on in this world are the people who get up and look for the circumstances they want and if they can't find them, make them.

Three cheers for George Bernard, the Goal Seeker, Shaw!

Many people seem to consider the word *opportunity* to be some kind of mystical expression, a word that has meaning only to a chosen few who get the chance to experience its magic effect and results. Many associate *opportunity* with luck and gambling, say it is something you must wait for. What foolishness! You don't wait for an opportunity. You just go where it is and *wait on it*—hand and foot!

An opportunity is merely a favorable combination of circumstances. It starts with being in the right place at the right time. That could be luck, but more often it's a matter of *getting yourself* to the right place at the right time. From that point onward, all you need is the guts to make a move that will advance you toward your goal.

Sometimes an opportunity can be just the opposite—an *unfavorable* combination of circumstances that will force you to move. For example, it was apparent to me that I had gone as far as I could go with the lawn and garden distributor I worked for. He refused to expand and, to make it clear he wanted no more pressure from me, he reduced my bonus and held back a check I had earned as a sales incentive. So, I didn't wait for opportunity to knock. I went looking for it. I went to Kmart, which was one more step in the direction of my goal.

When you're out hunting opportunities, remember three things:

1. The opportunity you take advantage of today isn't your first and will not be your last or only opportunity. Opportunities come in all shapes and sizes. Some are so small you may hardly recognize them, but they all add up, so seize them. An opportunity is worth tending to, whether it moves you an inch or a mile closer to your goal. It's not the distance but the direction that matters.

2. Opportunities are like a gift horse. Don't look one in the mouth. Look it in the eyes and make sure they're open. Then mount that opportunity and ride the hell out of it.

3. Remember that all opportunities aren't gentle old nags. Some of the best ones are real bucking broncos.

I don't remember my ride at Kresge Kmart being very gentle. For nine years there, someone was always putting a burr under my saddle. If it was so rough, why didn't I get off? I stayed on because that horse was bucking and charging toward my goal. Also, I was learning a lot. The best way to learn incidentally, is to keep your eyes open. And if you've ever ridden a bronco, you *know* you'll keep your eyes open!

Who is a Goal Seeker?

Goal seekers are folks who are fed up with the rest of the complacent complainers around them. They are impatient with the slow pace that has been set for their progress towards the better things in society; they hold no brief for "rules" that bar advancement until a certain age or seniority is attained, simply because "that's the way it was done in the past." Goal seekers are aware. They know that anything is possible if they are willing to put forth the mental and physical effort. They believe that change is inevitable only if *they* institute that change. A goal seeker is a person who *knows* in his heart what he wants from this short life of ours and is willing to pay the price. The goal seeker never worries about the mundane obstacles others use as excuses to cover up their insecurities: race, nationality, religion, age, sex, or restricted education. These are

obstacles only if you think they are. If I have just described you, welcome aboard! It's not exactly an exclusive club, is it?

The Holy Bible was full of goal seekers. The founding fathers of
this nation were also among their ranks. Men in the early labor
movements were excellent examples, too, along with the giants
of the automotive industry, and many athletes, scholars, artists,
and authors. The list even includes the "kingpins" of the crime
syndicates.

If you haven't gotten the picture by now, if you haven't discovered
what all of these examples of men and women have in common,
then I would suggest that you put this book down and forget about
organizing a team because you are not a true goal seeker.

For those of you who recognize that these were people who were
not satisfied with their lot in life and who successfully made changes
in their situations, read on! You are now on your way to the tryouts.

Now, before anyone gets on a high horse because I grouped religion, politics, crime and business all together, let me state that I
am *not* implying that everyone has similar goals. In a moralistic
sense you can say that goals differ in quality, because some persons
crusade for good and some for evil, but goals never differ in the way
they are successfully achieved. I am merely pointing out that each
type of goal seeker cited was out to change, improve, and *control*
his or her situation. Sometimes this also meant controlling the situations of those around them through implementing a plan and positive action.

Again, let's turn to *Webster* for another underlined-in-red
definition:

> **Goal:**   the terminal point of a race, the end toward which an effort
> is directed.

> **Seeker:**   one who perceives keenly.

There you've got it! Those two definitions together describe my
interpretation of who and what a goal seeker is.

"That's just a fancy name for a status seeker," you might say. Well,
if that's the way you see it, then quit now while you are able, because if you continue you'll only be fooling yourself. When the going
gets rough you'll have to struggle doubly hard to hedge your bet
and find a reasonable excuse which will get you out through the
back door.

Status has to do with relative rank in a hierarchy based upon
prestige. What we are talking about are tangible goals. Instead of

asking you to underline here, let me give you one more reminder about goals. Goals, to goal seekers as we have defined them, can be ascribed a *value* and that value will be individual and unique to the goal seeker whose goal it is. No one has the right to set a goal or goals for another human being.

When I am asked to give examples of successful goal seekers, I invariably mention Bob Kennedy, Dinah Shore, Jessie Jackson, Ben Fauber, Dutch Leonard, Tyson Tildon, Merv Griffin, Dick Clark, Chris Duffey, H.B. Cunningham, Rocky Meldrum, John Campbell, Ted Turner, Phil Donahue and a slug of others. Some of these goal seekers you will recognize by name or because their feats have made news. Others may be strangers to you because they accomplished their goals in a way that gained success without gathering headlines. They did it quietly. Nevertheless, all those I've named had a burning intensity. They all sought and found an opportunity to go somewhere others had not yet ventured, or to reach goals at which others had failed.

Bob Kennedy is an excellent example of a low-key goal seeker. He was totally dedicated to both his career and his family—which goes to prove a point I will repeat later on, that a goal seeker is not a workaholic and can be selfish and generous at the same time. This Bob Kennedy was not the President's brother. He was host of a highly successful morning talk show in Chicago on which I was a regular weekly guest. The show was called *Kennedy & Company*. As a rule, when you think of a TV or radio personality, you think of a tall, tanned, handsome guy with a deep baritone voice and a toothpaste-commercial smile. Well, Bob Kennedy was very short. He looked like a character out of a Norman Rockwell painting. His voice was nothing special but he had a pixie smile that was so good it should have been patented. He was one of the best interviewers I have ever watched or worked with. Bob's goal was to become a national celebrity on the network and own a home in Rye, New York, like his idol, Edward R. Murrow. Bob Kennedy had come to the American Broadcasting station, WLS-TV, in Chicago from a radio station in Boston. He put his plan into action, working hard to build a reputation as a good, spontaneous, on-camera interviewer. He did his homework thoroughly and built a team that worked as hard as he did—not only to please the audience, but to make guests on the show happy. As a result, when ABC-TV decided to go head-to-head with NBC's popular *Today Show*, launching a program called

Good Morning America, it came as a great surprise to most of the industry when an unknown, little, warm, sincere, dedicated, and totally professional—Bob (Goal Seeker) Kennedy—was named as the host.

But TV history buffs may say, "Wait a minute! If Bob Kennedy was selected, how come David Hartman opened the show?"

The answer to that one is that some of the greatest performances are never seen on television. Bob did reach his goal.

He bought the home in Rye, New York. He started rehearsals for *Good Morning America*. But it got harder and harder for Bob Kennedy to keep flashing that pixie smile. For months he had been suffering back pains, but put them down to muscle tears from his regular jogging. He applied heating pads and liniment and kept on working. Before the new show was to debut, Bob and his wife, Bev, took a long planned trip to Spain. The back pain persisted, even when he quit jogging. On his return, he saw a doctor and was told he had cancer of the spine. Still, he went back to work to claim his goal. He kept his illness secret, determined to overcome it. But, hard as he tried, he never made it to air time. He died.

Bob Kennedy did everything a goal seeker should do. He set his goal, scouted the opposition, picked his team, devised a game plan and played it to a win. However, you are well aware, time runs out in all of our games someday.

Who is a goal seeker? All of us are to some extent, but few ever recognize it.

There are certain professions that automatically attract goal seekers. People in the entertainment field—stage, screen, radio and TV—as well as writers, athletes, investment bankers, surgeons, test pilots, and race-car drivers all have the goal-seeking instincts as part of their makeup. As I tell audiences around the world, such people also have in common the attitude that they will never allow destiny to be their career driver, nor fate their footman.

Demotions and Lateral Moves are a Career Injustice . . .

If ever there were an incentive to become a goal seeker, it is demotion on your job or a lateral move, no matter what the reason.

Many organizations feel they are being generous and thoughtful in moving an employee who fails to perform in an assigned area of management into a subordinate job, rather than dismissing him. In fact, demotion is cruel, cowardly and, in many cases, selfish. I once heard a senior member of management in one of the big three auto firms make the statement, "Someone has to do the dirty work, why not let it be the losers?"

If you are not happy at what you do, or the job is beyond your mental or physical capabilities, get the hell out! Don't let anyone keep you down, set a goal, design a game plan, pick a team and be a winner.

For those of you who have used this practice as managers, why not just make out-placement available? It will be kinder.

If I Only Knew then What I Know Now

There isn't one person alive who hasn't made this statement aloud or to themselves on more than one occasion. The truth of the matter is that as an adult, young or old, we have the ability to judge any and every situation or opportunity and make a rational decision as to whether we should or shouldn't proceed. If we fail, we invoke the old "If I only knew then" cliché. If we succeed, we might well brag that we never had any doubt as to the outcome. I have found over the years that if I list all of the advantages of taking a particular action in the pursuit of a goal on paper and then make a similar list of the disadvantages, and then asking council of my team members for additions to either or both lists, adding up the total of each list gives me that insight needed to continually win (since I merely take the action dictated by the longest list). The moral of this advice is simple: Take advantage of all the things you learned along the way now! Then is *now*, and the future will only be pleasant and profitable memories if you make those thens your goals today.

Seniority Should Never be Mistaken for Security or Promotions

With the advent of the early retirement ploy, which is being used to get around the age discrimination suits, many of you may find that you are back in the competitive market involuntarily and you must find work or income to supplement your comfortable less-than-expected retirement income. If you begin now to think like and act like a goal seeker, adding to your present knowledge through adult education programs in marketing, advertising, computer programming and word processing, sales or any other subject that you feel might help you in the future, then you'll always be prepared for a new and profitable opportunity, no matter how it is thrust upon you.

If You Can't Admit You're Selfish, You Can't Win

Those were words of tennis superstar Chris Evert after she withdrew from the 1978 Virginia Slims Tournament.

As you play, be selfish because if you can't feel completely selfish, you can't win. "Selfish? What about so-called team effort?" you may ask. Let me explain.

There's a certain kind of selfishness I have in mind. If you have the right kind of selfishness, you should, can, and will earn the reputation of being a generous person, which as you'll see, won't be in contradiction of the selfishness I advocate.

The time for generosity is when victory's yours. Then, and only then, you'll share the spoils you've gained. Along the way, be selfish with the riches right at hand, namely your time. Time is precious, and it cannot be wasted. The penalty will be prohibitive: you'll lose the whole game.

Likewise, once you start to run a play just called, you must concentrate on that play, and that play only. Take it from me, there will be no time for any distractions.

The goal seeker is a highly disciplined individual, quarterbacking a highly tuned team of specialists. A wandering mind at the wrong moment could cause a loss that turns out to be fatal, and any goal seeker worthy of the name knows it. There's a parable my Grandma Putt passed on to me that applies here:

> When you were born, God filled the bank of life for you and then said, Okay, you can spend your lifetime anyway you want and on anything you want. The only reservations to your freedom of choice and

action are the ten rules I carved in stone and gave to Moses to pass
on to you.

Sounds like a pretty good deal? Remember one thing. God in all
of his generosity (and you'd really better take me seriously here)
decided not to give you the key or the bank book for your account.
None of us knows how much time he has, so be selfish, use time
wisely, make every minute count.

It seems to me that what Chris Evert was saying was that the time
and effort it would have taken to win that tournament would have
been wasted. Winning that particular contest was not her immediate goal. Physical and mental rest appeared to be the best investment at the time. Selfish? Certainly!

Goals are Plural

Goal seeking is not a function of age. Any person who sincerely
wants something and who is willing to put the necessary planning
and effort into getting it is a goal seeker. Children can be goal seekers. For example, a child who wants a new bicycle and earns the
money to buy it is a goal seeker—and an achiever. Another child
who wants a bike and successfully steals the model of his or her
choice is also a goal seeker—and achiever. Goal seeking is not limited to the guys with the white hats. Remember that.

You can have many goals in mind at the same time. I have my
ultimate goal, my annual goal, and monthly, weekly, daily and "at
hand" goals. When any of the six goals have been scored, including
the ultimate, I set new ones.

Play Life for the Fun of It

I liken goals and goal seeking to a football game. From here on, we'll
think in terms of football, a sport that every American can relate to
by choice or default.

The ultimate goal of a football team is to win the game. To win,
the team must run up a lot of points. To make points, the team must
gain yardage. To gain yardage, the team must knock the defense on
their backsides, and to do that, the team or individual must decide

upon and carry out a plan. Each of these steps is a goal—not just winning the game, but running up points, gaining yardage, breaking the defense—and all of them must be kept in mind at once in order to succeed. If you think I'm oversimplifying, you're right! I do so with reason. Set simple plans for yourself and your team. Otherwise, you'll confuse yourself, not the opposition.

I'm often asked how I can keep so many projects going at the same time without getting everything mixed up. It's simple. They only look like a lot of different projects. The truth is that they're all the means to one end, my present ultimate goal.

When I put on that green suit for Kmart, I had an earlier ultimate goal. I wanted a regular spot on all three major media—radio, TV and newspapers. Now, for an ex-cop with no formal training in any medium, that was one hell of a goal. Goals, plural, I mean. But taking them on one at a time, I made radio my first play. Every day, driving from store to store, I'd listen to my car radio—and analyze what I heard. I tuned in one show in particular called *Ask Your Neighbor*, a three-hour show hosted by Bob Allison.

Folks would call in with problems about household subjects like, "How do you get ballpoint pen ink out of a janitor's shirt?" Or, "Who has a recipe for chocolate sponge cake?" Then someone else would phone in the answer. I noticed that when questions came in about plants or gardening, there was seldom an answer. Well, that silence was my opportunity! I'd make a screaming stop at the nearest pay phone and call the station saying, "This is Mr. Grow-It-All," and answer the question. Pretty soon, listeners would call and ask Bob Allison to ask Mr. Grow-It-All about this or that. Well, Allison didn't know who I was or where to find me, but I would call in and answer. For about two weeks I was sort of like Clark Kent as Superman. Who was this mysterious Mr. Grow-It-All? Then one morning, driving by a shopping center from which the show was originating, I heard the first question out of the bag. It was about house plants! I drove my wildly decorated van right up to the broadcast booth and all six feet and four inches of Mr. Grow-It-All in his kelly green suit alighted to face one totally shocked open-mouthed announcer who said, "Folks, you won't believe this but there really *is* a Mr. Grow-It-All!" Shortly thereafter I became a regular member of the show. I recorded daily segments with it for more than ten years.

I knew that once I had established my authority in one medium, the others would come easier, so I simply called the *Detroit Free*

Press and asked for the man in charge of features. I was connected with Bill Baker (no relation) and I told him I wanted to write a column on gardening and plants. He said, "Send me a sample." I did. That clinched medium number two!

Next, I was to prove without a doubt that opportunity knocks often if you'll just answer the door. A TV producer had heard me on the radio and wondered what I'd look like on TV. He didn't wonder long. When I showed up in the green suit and the Growmobile, I was hired on the spot.

Please realize that while all this was going on, I still had my hands full with my store responsibilities, but everything was paying off promotionally and financially. Mr. Grow-It-All was the name and gardening was his game.

Just make sure that *your* game plan is properly laid out so that each play leads to the next. Get your goals coordinated. That way, no matter how many you have going at one time, they won't get mixed up and make you drop the ball.

Part I
First Quarter

Before you begin to play, there is one more aspect of the goal seeking game you must understand. To do so, you have to discard an old idea that has received a lot of undeserved mileage—I mean that bit about it's not whether you win or lose but how you play the game.

It's bull! Only losers think that way. Winning is the only thing. How you play does make a difference, of course, because if you play the right way—to win—you won't lose. Playing to win means playing for keeps. The opposition will feel your presence the minute they open the locker room door. And that's the place to separate the amateurs from the professionals. The amateur plays for fun, the professional plays for gold. It's that simple!

Chapter 2

Profile of a Goal Seeker

Let me make one thing perfectly clear. You won't win them all in the beginning, but don't be discouraged and give up. Just learn from your mistakes, practice harder and come back for a rematch.

Most people lose because they go into the game with the idea that they might lose. I have never ever attempted a goal with the remotest idea that I could lose. A loss to me is as big a surprise as it is to my opponents.

I will make the statement later on that you don't play for the spectators' benefit, but for your own selfish motives—your goals. Winning sure makes it more pleasant to enter a room where others know you won!

Back in the early 60s there was a small bar and restaurant on Detroit's west side called Charley Harrison's Manor. Nothing fancy but one of the most popular watering troughs for business, political and sports figures. Charley's was a great place to celebrate. I also found it an ideal spot to relax an opponent.

On one occasion, I went to Charley's to celebrate scoring a goal. I had acquired a marketing business and had invited the owner and three of my teammates to share in the victory celebration.

I arrived at Charley's before my guests did and was stopped by a loudmouth who yelled at me from the bar, "Hey, Green Bean! You trying to go big time with pros? Well you don't have a chance to take on our line!" That turkey, believe it or not, was the marketing manager of the firm I had just acquired. He didn't know about my deal because his boss hadn't been able to find him for three days—thanks to the successful maneuvering of one of my players who took him skiing where there were no phones.

Well, I just let him go on with his tirade. He said I should have stayed a cop. At that moment, his boss and two of my players entered. The boss, thinking I had invited this character, rushed over to tell him about our new arrangements. Still standing in the same spot in which I had taken his tongue lashing, I watched the color drain from his face.

I then walked over and asked him to join us. Would he care to discuss his new responsibilities?

When you are the winner, you can afford to be generous!

Can't Goals Box You In?

Goals can't box you in if you make darned sure that your goals are placed in the right order with a reasonable time allotted for the accomplishment of each one. You will understand this better as we go on. There are some considerations to ponder before you make a serious selection of any given goal. I call it the need-and-desire syndrome, and I am the first to admit that this is a controversial area. Need is a dependency factor and dependency factors tend to place a person in a highly vulnerable position relative to decisions. The need factor tends to increase indecision and also tends to influence judgment to the point where overly aggressive and often unnecessary chances are taken.

The desire factor (more commonly called the *want factor*) stimulates creative tendencies. Desire can stimulate aggression, too, but operating from desire rather than from need, places less pressure on you. You're more free to think.

When you consider going for a goal, weigh it against this need-want factor. I have both kinds of goals, but let me tell you that a goal seeker's game with a preponderance of desire factors is easier and more fun than any game based on need goals.

I find that the biggest impediment for many persons is lack of a direction for their creative activities. In one sense of the word, goals are a self-imposed box for keeping your efforts concentrated, to discourage "scatter-braining," flitting from one interest to another. To that extent, goals *do* box you in—in the *winner's* box!

You Can be a Part-time Goal Seeker

I know a good number of successful goal seekers who are satisfied, for the most part, with their position and the progress in society they've made. They acquired most the material things they want. But from time to time they find themselves desiring something out of the ordinary, so they plunge into a full-fledged goal seeker's game.

Another full-time goal seeker and I were discussing a mutual friend who plays only part-time. We agreed that as long as we have known this party he has always made satisfying progress because he practices the basic goal seeker's philosophy. However, he does not want to own or run the whole show. He does every job he is assigned to the best of his ability and does not hesitate to speak up when something is beyond his present scope. Still he's a holy terror when it comes to playing a goal seeker's game. I know. I have played for him on more than one occasion.

The Full-time Goal Seeker

The full-timer is a person who is self-motivated in a highly competitive society and who has many diverse interests. The full-timer loves a challenge—and note I said a *challenge* and not a *dare*. Dares are non-profitable and often dangerous. A professional full-time goal seeker is often referred to as an entrepreneur, a person who organizes and promotes activities. Entrepreneurs also manage and assume all risks.

A full-time professional goal seeker never needs flim-flams or scams and wouldn't be caught dead taking advantage of anyone who was not capable of defending his profession mentally or physically!

The Goal Seeker and the Opportunist

When you decide to become a goal seeker, you will be called all kinds of names: mercenary bastard, money-hungry s.o.b., social climber, or power-crazed monster. More often than not you will hear the ultimate epithet. You will be called "an opportunist." And to some extent that will be a true description. Technically, an opportunist is one who takes advantage of opportunities and circumstances, but here is where the resemblance ends. Your principles are the rules by which you will play and by which you will be judged. Without regard for the ultimate consequences, you might win the game, but you'd lose respect for yourself.

So, let them call you an opportunist and then surprise them by winning fairly. Corny as it sounds, that old sticks 'n stones ditty fits this situation nicely.

Goals Can be Personal

I don't want to confuse the issue and yet I want you to know all there is to the game of goal seeking. Earlier I made the statement that accomplishments are measured by material wealth. That sounds crass, but in the end wealth is our yardstick for success. However, there are a great many things which influence our ability to gain wealth. The three most important are health, love, and education. I can't be hypocritical about education. The fact that many of us who are professional goal seekers have limited educations doesn't make lack of education the "in" thing.

A goal seeker values education. Whether Ph.D. or grammar school graduate, my kind of player is forever hungry for knowledge. Those of us who graduated from the "University of Hard Knocks" would gladly exchange that curriculum for a conventional college education, but you'll still find us in night school or the library, reading, studying, making every effort to learn. Get all the education you can and then keep studying the rest of your life. Some of the easiest guys to beat are the ones who earn a diploma and then never learn another thing after they leave college. Knowledge is like lettuce. It wilts if you don't use it . . . and you have to replace it with fresh stuff daily!

If love sounds funny in a game that seems as hard-nosed as this, then you are mistaken. If you don't have someone with whom to share your joys and accomplishments, you will be a very hollow person. Most goal seekers are warm and outgoing with their loved ones—and not because of a guilty conscience over the time and effort they put into the pursuit of their goals. I don't feel any such pangs, nor do my wife and five children complain any more about me than they might if I were just another Joe who bowls in two leagues a week.

Health was listed first, but is last to be discussed because it's the point I want you to remember longest. Your personal health is the number one consideration in how involved you can get in the fast-paced, high-pressure, mentally fatiguing game of goal seeking. Enroll in your local health club—I mean it! Both your appearance and your physical condition will have a bearing on the outcome of more than one series of plays.

Next, alcohol and drugs have no place in the goal seeker's life. I'm not saying you can't drink. What I am saying is that if a drink inhibits you from making a sound decision, don't drink. And, never drink when you are (1) listening to reports, (2) making an offer, or (3) negotiating for the thing that is your goal.

As for drugs and medicines, you'll have plenty of ups and downs without taking uppers or downers. Even legal drugs and medicines, if not prescribed for your health by your physician, are a no-no. Personally, I don't even take aspirins, I don't believe in fooling around with that old body chemistry.

Remember, I spent some time as a police officer around narcotics addicts. I saw enough grief to know that dope could never be a temptation for me, but alcohol was another story. Booze almost became a problem, but I admitted it at the same time I discovered what a goal seeker was. My first game was against alcohol, a habit I had acquired, and losing would have kept me from ever achieving my goal. I won, but it's a game I'll never stop playing.

So you see, some goals can be very private and personal.

Don't Let the "If I Were You" Ever Influence Your Choice of Goals

There is probably no one who has not had a well-meaning friend, member of the family or just an acquaintance offer us this useless introduction to a bit of unsolicited advice: "If I were you . . . " Don't be influenced by that. To begin with, the people who say, "If I were you" are *not* you, so they cannot judge what they would do if they *were* you and faced with the same circumstances or the same mental, physical or financial pressures. They can only give you their *opinion* of what they might do at the present moment and within circumstances as they understand them. I am not advocating the refusal of counseling or sincere advice, nor am I saying that it is wrong to solicit advice from trusted, knowledgeable persons. But I can never recall hearing anyone whose advice I trusted say, "If I were you." Men and women who have your best interests at heart will never use those words as openers. Your goals are so important to you that you should never allow anyone to influence them by proposing to think for you.

The Goal Seeker Picks His Own Train and Hopes All Others Made the Right Connection

A longtime acquaintance of mine had set a career goal for himself. He designed a game plan and then worked his tail off. He liked the work he did. He felt that the firm he worked for was generous in its pay scale and that his chances for advancement were restricted only by his own efforts. He took night courses to strengthen his knowledge of the job. He followed his game plan to the letter and won far more than he had hoped for—vice presidency, stock bonus, super salary, and a dream assignment. The dream, however, turned out to be a nightmare because the assignment that would advance his career this major step was in another state.

You guessed it, perhaps? His wife refused to move and leave her house, family and friends. The terrible part of this story is that the wife knew this could happen, but she never said a word about it during all the years her husband bent his efforts toward his goal. She was secretly betting he wouldn't make it. A sad thought, indeed, to think that someone you love has been betting against you.

That man's firm was the kind that made an offer once. If you declined, you were written off. Don't think this policy is unusual, it's common practice in major corporations.

My old friend and his wife had some long and serious discussions. She suggested he commute!

Well, you must know how the story ends by now. These two found they no longer wanted to ride on the same train. It turned out best for my friend. He is now the chairman of the board of that company and she is remarried—for the third time.

Since a good marriage is a give-and-take proposition, it's a good idea for each partner to know where the other wants to go. In marriage no one party can be a constant taker. The goal seeker considers this before making goal decisions, or applying for a marriage license.

You Can't Run with a Millstone around Your Neck

John is home every night of the week at six o'clock and he paints the bedrooms every June. Gladys is his millstone. If she doesn't feel well, he takes a sick day.

I'm sure you get the picture. If you are a serious goal seeker, you will almost certainly be exposed to a few millstones who could keep you from passing the milestones. Oh don't look so smug, ladies. It has a flip side, too.

In general, a goal seeker will spend more cumulative time with his family than will the average progressor. But when the goal seeker is in the middle of a game, he's not the most reliable partner on the domestic front, and the local handymen, maids, and tradespeople will get their share of his wealth. There will be times when you can't call time out to change a light bulb, pour liquid plumber down the drain, or paint a bedroom ceiling. It can become a real problem if you let it—so take care of your primary responsibilities first and then make sure you do your share when time permits (between games).

The Person Who Wants You to Fail is the One Closest to You

This statement will raise an eyebrow or two. Men are the worst—married men. It is no secret that in a family in which both partners work, the husband resents a wife's income or management status if it comes close to, or rises above his own. On the other hand, most women want their husbands' income to be high enough to provide them with the life style they require, but they do not want him to progress creatively to the point where he may consider expanding his independence.

What's behind this begrudging attitude of spouses? A feeling of insecurity! If you are to be a successful goal seeker, you will not have time to waste worrying about whether your wife or husband is getting ahead of you. The same goes for brothers, sisters, best friends and, in many cases, fathers and sons. In today's society, where more than fifty percent of all families have two working principals, an additional strain is put on the marriage when one is promoted and must move from one city to another. You and your partner are individual, independent, creatures and each should have the admiration for the progress of the other.

Chapter 3

Choose Your Team Carefully

Some readers will find fault with my comparing life's career and personal efforts to a "game." I don't understand why. A game is something you play for a stake. It's a gamble. The stake we go for in everything we do is success—and the gamble is whether you will succeed. Most efforts are made individually, but from time to time we find that we want to include others in our plan to accomplish a goal. Any time more than one person is involved in achieving a goal, it will be necessary to coordinate all efforts. This is called team-work. When it's necessary for you to require assistance to attain your goal, then you'd better make sure that those whose services you request are familiar with team play. It may be a bit difficult in the beginning for you to understand why you don't just ask your friends, relatives, or the nearest local businessman for assistance.

Read on, you will soon understand.

Don't Start Out with Secrets

Over the years I have witnessed this exact situation many times and in different ways. A former partner of mine in the police department was an excellent artist with oils, water colors, pastels, inks—any material you could draw or paint with. His *dream* was to open a studio and make a living with his talent, but his wife discouraged this on the grounds that artists were all drunks who could not make a decent living. My partner began by selling pieces of his work here and there and putting the money in a safety deposit box. Then he began displaying work in restaurants, bars and gift shops on a consignment basis, selling more and more and squirreling more and more away in the lock-box. An opportunity arose quite unexpectedly for this very talented man to get a small retail shop on a main street where he could frame his work as well as paint. More success followed. But . . . then the proverbial stuff hit the fan and a police department corruption investigation began. You guessed it! The results of the success came to light . . . don't prejudge yet folks . . . my partner kept great books and gave receipts for all purchases, and he was exonerated from any corruption. But his wife and uncle were not so understanding. They both thought he was holding out, and what she didn't get in the divorce, the IRS got.

You Don't Need Marital Permission Just an Understanding

This may seem like an extension to the rule about not starting out with secrets. If you are to be a successful goal seeker, you will have all the facts before you make any decision, be it buying a new dress, pair of shoes, sport coat or suit. You are not a child. You do not need to ask permission to make such purchases, and you don't need to ask your husband if you can get a job or go back to school for further training. You do not need permission to set your goals, either.

Don't Settle for Second Stringers

We all know people who are pretty good in their jobs, occupations and careers. Emphasis is on the word *pretty*, rather than *good*. The best anyone can ever say about these folks is that one of them could be a "pretty good choice." Now what that means to me is that they will do a job for you but you'll always have to keep your eye on them to make sure the job gets done. I seldom expect the "pretty goods" to do anymore than is asked of them. Nor do I expect them to be imaginative or creative. If a goal is worth working for, then it's worth going after with a first-string team. Well now, you may say, "What if I can't afford the best team in the specialty I need? Won't I have to settle for some players I can afford?" The answer is yes, but price doesn't necessarily determine the quality of the player. It just means you must look harder for a qualified player with the tag that says "good" who will play for what you can afford to pay.

In my day, I've found some super rookies!

Honor the "Black List"

Since this is a book of basic fundamentals, I must include this warning: Never, under any circumstances, are you to recruit or accept the services of a convicted thief or cheat. If it is even rumored that a player has a habit of clipping or constantly working on the face mask, check it out, and if there is any doubt, don't touch him with a ten-foot pole. All you need is to have a goal called back for a personal foul. It could be devastating. In addition to the call-back, you will have lost additional ground and time. And now the defense knows exactly what you're contemplating. Besides, you're bushed from the run. There are other things that can get a player on the black list besides dishonesty—viciousness, for instance.

Make Sure All Your Players are Strong on the Three-P Strategy

Pride, Patience and *Persistence*. A player who is proud of the position he or she plays and who plays it to the best of his ability is going to be strong and totally reliable. A player who is patient and listens to the call doesn't get flustered and break too soon. Such a player will block the opposition, protect you, and give you the time you need. Odds are he'll fluster the defense with his coolness, causing them to buck and give you some free yardage.

Persistance is the toughest quality to come by, but you need it most when everything is against you. Quitting is the easiest thing in the world, but if you refuse to quit and try one more time, you're bound to break through. You may be battered, but you'll also be bettered by the experience.

There is nothing wrong with taking a time-out to go over to the bench and talk to the scouts—there may be something they overlooked in their report to you.

- Cover the ball.
- Avoid fumbles.

Pretty obvious, isn't it?

Paid to Play

In the game of goal seeking, nobody plays for the fun of it. Everyone expects to get paid in some way, if not in money, then in services, favors or a piece of the action. So make damned sure all of the contracts are in before the game starts. If you wait until the end, you just might find out you played for nothing. A tie is not bankable or spendable. If the price is too high for a player you want to sign, negotiate. Or, look for another player. By the way, there are plenty of good free agents for any business game.

If you are having a problem relating to my football analogy, let's try another one to make this paid-to-play point. Let's say a man who runs for mayor, governor, president or senator needs a team and must pay that team (or pay off, usually with jobs or appointments). Some of his players may think they are worth more than he's willing to pay. He must, therefore, decline their services.

A run for the presidency of a company is one hell of a goal seeker's game to watch. Every player charges his price to keep the quarterback from getting killed on the way.

One last word—and this will affect the pay schedule: Goal seeking is never played on a sunny bright day on Astroturf. It is played in the cold rain on a muddy field. Always!

Share the Wealth

Now let's set a budget by adding up the cost of playing the game. You must take all things into consideration. First, what is the total cost of the team in cash outlay or future favors? Second, what will the goal, when achieved, return on the cost of play?

On more than one occasion, I have delayed a game until a later date because the return on investment just didn't make sense. Always remember—don't vary your strategy for the fun of it. And never ask your players to play for nothing, because it takes just as much time and effort and the chances for injury are the same as when you play for real. This may suggest a contradiction. It isn't.

On occasion, I've had the services of a superstar offered when I least expected it. In one such instance, when I was involved in securing private labeling for a line of consumer products from a major manufacturer, I stated flatly I could not afford the superstar and could see no service I could ever offer him in repayment. So he said, "If you can use my services, I would like to see you win this game because I like your style." Well, we won that one easily and when I tried to pay him he refused, wouldn't take a thing.

I put that one in my *owed* book but have never been able to close the book. His final remark was, "I learned something from your strategy." So my question is, did I pay, and did he play for a fee or free?

We Don't Have a Taxi Squad, Just Specialists

Once you've decided upon a goal and have started to recruit your team, make a list of all the defensive obstacles that stand between you and your goal. If your goal is launching a new product, for example, the obstacles can be package design, market demographics, media (TV, radio and print), marketing strategy, sales force, etc. Make a list of them. Then list the names of all the pros you know who are specialists in each of those areas. Ask your scouts to add their suggestions to your list, and always remember to use the philosophy of "the richest man in Babylon," which says that if you want bread baked, go to a baker, bricks laid, go to a bricklayer. Without the right specialists, you're licked before you start.

Make Sure You and Your Team are Physically Fit, Mentally Alert, and Morally Aggressive

This sounds a little like the Boy Scout Pledge, but it's not out of place in the context of this book. Between us adults, it is very much in place and of the utmost importance in the goal seeker's life. When you were a child, your health, education, and moral training were supervised by adults. When you left that influence and environment, your attitudes and behavior suddenly became *your* responsibility. All of us, after leaving our well-supervised nests, can become neglectful. Free to run our own lives, we form new habits, and not always good ones.

When you select persons for your team, make sure that to the best of your knowledge they will be physically able to last out the game you're playing to win. Perhaps a potential player has an illness that could be aggravated by the stress game. It would be unfair to that person and unsafe for you, to ask him or her to play. Neither of you should risk a critical time. Hiring a known practicing alcoholic is an absolute no-no.

Then there is your own physical condition to consider. If you're not feeling well at the time a new goal comes up, it's best to postpone the game until later. I learned that lesson the hard way.

Having just come out of a hard-fought game—promoting my book and doing three different radio and TV shows coast-to-coast—I had won, but it drained me. Another challenging game offered itself just as I was trying to put myself together. Another TV program! Back onto the field I went. My trainer was furious. (My trainer is my beautiful and dedicated wife, mother of five fine children.) She suggested I go to the team physician for a check-up but I declined and went back to work on selecting a new team. I asked for scouting reports, worked out a fresh game plan and took the kickoff. The game was going all our way. I mean it looked like a shutout, but three weeks from the goal I collapsed from physical exhaustion, alone in a motel room in Minneapolis. I contracted pneumonia and nearly didn't make it home to the trainer. We won that one, finally, but I was out of the game—and almost out of this world—for several months.

Annual physical check-ups are absolutely necessary. I go every six months. I don't care how good you *think* you feel. Female players are even more likely to overlook this point. Take it from one who missed and damned near lost everything.

When I say you have to keep mentally awake, it sounds kind of funny, but when a player forgets a play or you get sacked for running into a wall, it won't seem so funny, not to mention the damage in lost yardage. If a person is involved in a personal situation such as a divorce or there is business pressure which will affect his or her concentration, pick another player.

The words, "morally aggressive," may sound contradictory, but nice guys actually win more than they lose. If you and your team have a reputation for clean, hard playing, the opposition will know it has its hands full.

Pick Players, Not Spectators

When you approach a prospective player, explain the goal and the game plan. Agree on a price and then observe closely during the game to make sure that he or she is contributing. You may find you've got just another warm body out on the field. If so, what you really have on your hands is a spectator and not a player, so you'd better go over the conditions of the contract and make a change. It may cost you at the time, but it's worth it in the long run. As for the spectator who shilled you into thinking he was a player, remember the Black List. This breed deserves it.

Don't Overload the Roster

In the game of goal seeking, even though I'm comparing it to football, neither you nor the defense have to use eleven players per side, or any other set number. Once you've determined the basic size of your team, you may need two or three additional players (specialists). But quality, not size of team, is what counts. I have on occasion taken on too many players and put double squads in the field. But I won't do it again. Extra players cost you and they get edgy on the bench. You can always add players when needed, as sometimes happens. In one of the toughest business games I ever played, I had nine players up against a defense of four. The four men who controlled the goal I was seeking, a business I wanted to acquire, were so strong I needed all nine to overcome their defense.

One Player Per Family

I don't think this needs much explanation. I'm being a hard nose, but I've been through the family thing too many times and have learned that if it's not nipped in the bud it can screw up the whole team.

As the team owner and playing quarterback, I select a player for his or her proven talent. When it's time to play it's time to play, I want you on the field with your own head on your shoulders—not your wife's, your husband's, your father's, your big brother's or your mother's. And if you have a problem relative to the game, don't discuss it with anybody else but the team, damn it! That old World War II expression "Loose lips sink ships" is a good watchword for any goal seeker, all the time. Here's another good rule: don't take business to bed or to the dinner table. Your plans should only be discussed on a "need-to-know" basis only with those involved, not as casual conversation with the noninvolved.

Exceptions? Well, yes. I have had brothers, sisters, husband-wife combinations and father-son pairs on my team but they were recruited for their expertise and paid to play. That's the difference.

Keep Your Eyes on the "Gofers"

For those of you needing a definition, the word *gofer* refers to a person who hangs around a team, a group of people, musicians, actors, politicians, and other activities or notables. Many of them are pathetic. They go for coffee, run all sorts of errands, and often bear the brunt of a lot of jokes and tricks.

I will not allow any "gofers" near me or my team at any time and if I see or hear of a player using their dubious services, I find a new player.

The "gofer" is not always the kind of person you might think. Some are rich and some are poor, some are big and some are small. What they lack in common is guts enough to be a player. They get their kicks just associating with the players. For the most part, they're innocent cowards but sometimes their weaknesses can be your opponent's strength. The opposition can slide in a ringer on you. That's it, folks: a spy! I've seen whole games go down the tube because a gofer got inside and heard it all. For example, a friend of mine was acquiring property at a small lake that was surrounded by what looked like dense woods and brush. There didn't appear to be any shoreline and the lake bottom was considered too weedy for recreational use. The truth was that the foliage was soft scrub, easy and inexpensive to remove, and the appearance of weedy bottom was only a reflection of the shore brush, which also covered a fifteen-foot-deep shoreline. My friend had hired a young man to clean his offices after school. As it turned out, the boy was the ncphew of a competing developer. Within two weeks, my friend's project was destroyed when the cleaning boy's uncle purchased two pieces of property needed for access to the lake. As a policeman, I arrested characters with more morals than that. So I say to you, if you spot a gofer, you tell him to GO FAR!

Don't Fall For the "I Think You Ought To" Trap

You will have people coming out of the walls with suggestions that start with the words, "I think you ought to . . . " These people are attracted to you as a person who makes things happen. But don't let anyone talk you into a goal that won't benefit you and in which you don't have a sincere interest.

When you get an "I think you ought to" offer, you can test it with two questions. Ask that person, "Would you be interested in playing?" and "Would you be willing to fund the team at the prime rate?"

The answer is nearly always the same: No.

That's also your answer.

Chapter 4

Prepare Your Game Plan

I don't know many persons who would start on a long trip over strange territory without a mapped-out route. If they did, they would soon become lost. Time would be wasted. Life and life's goals are unfamiliar territory, too, so we must have a plan to follow so we do not get lost along the way. Also a timetable.

Almost without exception, men and women who are successful have a list or plan of what they must do—and when. They also make sure they know how they are going to go about accomplishing the goals they have assigned to themselves.

If you don't wish to get lost along life's way and waste the precious time which no one can replenish for you, then you must prepare a game plan for yourself that covers the entire trip as well as each individual goal. These plans are referred to as game plans and must be prepared with all of the care and consideration you can possibly give them. There's more to it than a brief note in your memory jogger.

How Can I Really Win?

If I say it's simple, I wouldn't be telling you the truth and truth is one of the key ingredients that makes this whole philosophy work. When you choose a goal, you have to be honest with yourself, asking, "Is this what I really want to do? Do I really want this goal?" Then make the most detailed plan you can, acquire the needed outside talent and run your tail off to accomplish it.

By now, some of you may be starting to think this game is too tough, too serious, that it may take more effort than you're willing to spend.

Well, goal seekers have just as much fun as anyone else. They bowl, dance, play cards, and go out like anyone else, but their productive, creative time is devoted to one purpose—attaining goals.

That doesn't mean you have to be gung ho all the time, either. Part of accomplishing mental goals involves reading, resting and planning in ways that contribute to your game. Remember: Success *is* fun. A better way of saying it is that fun itself is not the goal—just the reward for reaching the goal.

So, goal seekers can be fun seekers, too.

Pray to Win and Give Thanks When You Do

It sets me up when I hear spectators make fun of a team that says a little prayer before a game. I travel a lot so I'm not what a minister would call a good church-goer. I don't make it every Sunday. I go when my body and mind are there all for the same purpose, to communicate with the Spirit that made it possible to enjoy so many wonderful things and to go along being alive and healthy. Sometimes in a church, and more often alone in the woods or in my yard and garden, in a hotel room or my home workshop, it will hit me. We both know when we have something to talk about. I never try to fool myself that I can fool the Man. I know better. So, when I start a new game, I just let Him in on the game plan and trust He has time to observe. I know God loves winners—if they play by His rules. He has ten of them, called Commandments.

When you win, pay Him His commission, in a quiet and sincere way. Thank Him for what you have received and pray that He may help yet another who has not yet discovered what folks can do to help themselves. Praying for the sick or afflicted is another way of showing appreciation for your success.

The Goal Seeker and Religion

I am billed as a *motivator* and *energizationalist* by my lecture agent. My week is filled with the opportunity to inspire people to realize the opportunities available to them to reach their goals by utilizing their dormant abilities through imagination, ingenuity, and persistence. Men, women and college student groups pay to hear me, in hopes that they will learn of a secret formula for success.

But what about me? Where do I and others who have learned the secrets of goal seeking go for a recharge? I would love to say church. However, in nine out of ten cases, I would say we go to each other or among the honest and innocent children.

I am not a hypocrite. I have said that the Ten Commandments are the only rules. I do go to church, and my experience indicates that most other successful goal seekers do, too. I go to meditate, pause and give thanks for the opportunities we have been given to enjoy in life. Seldom, my colleagues say, do they hear an inspiring message from the pulpit. We are almost unaminous in our agreement that few men of the cloth have learned the technique of communication, the way to truly inspire their flock to face the next 534,800 seconds in the week in the way that our Greater Power has outlined in the Ten Commandments. If you would like proof of this, do a little survey of your own. Stand at the front door of your church and ask your fellow church members to repeat the Ten Commandments. You may be surprised to find out that well over ninety seven percent do *not* know the basic rules.

Everyone's goals are different. Ministers who have learned to charge their flocks' spiritual batteries are superstar goal seekers. I feel their goal is to guide me on the straight and narrow. I have stated that I am both a seeker of my own goals and a player on other teams, and the game of spiritual direction is one I gladly play.

Remember the Little Big Horn

Who can forget General Custer's last stand at the Little Big Horn? What most of us don't realize was that he was no longer a general when it happened, and there's probably no point in discussing his wisdom in dividing a six hundred man force into three groups and following a traditional military maneuver of flanking and charging.

During the Civil War, Custer, a fearless fighter for the Union Army, became known as "the boy general" soon after graduating at the bottom of his class from the U.S. Military Academy. After the war, he was returned to his permanent rank of captain, but George was a goal seeker with a game plan and a team to help him get back his rank of general.

He had guts, ambition and physical strength, but he violated one essential rule in attaining any goal. The rule is "Scout the opposition to know their weaknesses and strengths." Our former general, having worked his way back up to lieutenant colonel, got himself a command fighting Indians.

One day he spotted this nice little Indian camp alongside a pleasant little stream called the Little Big Horn. He was twelve or fifteen miles away, never closer, when he and his team decided on a game plan. The problem was that the game plan was drawn up on an assumption rather than fact. He assumed there were a thousand Indians—there were more than five thousand.

What I want you to remember and never forget is that the word *assume* breaks down into *ass-u-me* which means "it can make an ass of you and me"—and our team.

Remember this generalization and *you* can be a general!

Scout the Competition

I used to think ball clubs were wasting money when I'd hear about some retired player who became an advance scout. I thought it was a kind of charity, until I had the stuffing beat out of me because I didn't know about the competition in one of my biggest games— I lost an acquisition because I did not know the strength of my competition. "Scouting? That's spying, isn't it?" a friend asked. "Uh-huh," I replied.

When you are playing a game in which you bet your ass (and you've only got one) you had better make damned sure you know what the odds are on your losing it.

The scouts I hire are generally over fifty and retired, persons who were successful in their business, and appear loyal to my project (that is a calculated risk on my part).

Each scout must be an expert in a given field and know what to look for and where. I put my faith in their interpretation of the situation and design my game plan around that information—plus, of course, as much information as I can gather myself.

If you are getting into a situation in which your decisions on location or inventory or advertising depend on reliable information, either develop a scouting organization or don't even plan on showing up for the game. And, be honest with your scouts. Tell them what you are looking for, where you think your strength lies, and ask if they think your game plan is workable against the opposition. The scouts you use—their trades, professions and backgrounds—will vary from goal to goal.

The knowledge your scouts bring you will be as diversified as that of your players.

Put Your Plans on Paper

How many times have you had a real good idea that you wanted to write down but didn't have a piece of paper and pencil handy? Then rather than go out of your way to find those tools, you said, "I will remember it." And didn't. Or, maybe you were only able to remember part of it and tried to explain it to an associate, only to mess it up. No idea is ever as good as the moment when it's fresh, when it first pops into your mind.

When the idea for a game plan begins to develop in your mind concerning some particular goal, even if it's a future goal, write the idea down as completely as possible. Note when, where and what stimulated the idea for the plan and date your memo. There's something about writing things down that make ideas more clear even to yourself. Then, when you've got it captured in writing, you don't have to worry about losing it. You can go on to the next idea.

One way to be original, incidentally, is to include a few hard ways to do things. People hate work, so if you lay a fair amount of difficulty into some phase of your plan you can be sure few will try to imitate you.

How many times have you heard people say, examining someone else's plan, "That's an old trick?" Don't get caught with any old tricks. The people you're playing against are as determined to hold on to the turf as you are to take it away from them. If they know, or even suspect, your old tricks, you've had it.

When handing out assignments to players participating in one of your game plans, put them in writing too, so there can be no mistakes or reasons for excuses. Keep a copy of each player's assignment for quick reference when the action gets hot and heavy. Yes, sometimes things get so busy it's hard even for you yourself to remember what you told some player to do and you must know what each player is—or is not—supposed to be doing at all times.

As one of my teachers used to say, "Verbal instructions aren't worth the paper they're written on."

WRITE IT DOWN!

Innovate, Don't Copy!

When you are developing your strategy and devising your game plan, make every attempt to be original. If you must use a play that has been used before, make some change in it, because if it *has* been used before, someone can read it and make a defensive change that could cause you a loss or a turnover.

For example, when I was a police officer, we suspected a warehouse was being used as a drug-processing facility. The building had no windows on the ground floor and stood alone, so we could not get to the roof. It wouldn't do us any good to rush it, because the doors were so well reinforced that the people inside would have plenty of time to destroy the evidence. There was, however, a large trash container—a dumpster—in a bay that led to a chute inside the building. When the dumpster was removed to be emptied, we intercepted the truck and placed four officers inside the dumpster. It was inserted back into its bay right under the eyes of the lookouts. Our suspicions were confirmed. The place was a drug factory and, through innovation, we attained our goal of busting it.

Keep Your Ears Open for Members of the Defense with a Loser's Complex

There are people who, for one reason or another, are resigned to the fact that they are born losers. Nothing ever seems to go right for them on the job or in their personal life. Why do they think this way? Perhaps it's holding on to an unhappy marriage without the guts to admit it and stop living a miserable life. Or, maybe they have never progressed in the job market because of a negative attitude and lack of self-confidence. I can't begin to name all the reasons for the loser's complex, but there are lots of losers out there, and they can be helpful to you in your game. What I am advising is not cruel because a loser, after all, has nothing to lose. I'm advising you to look for loser symptoms among members of your opponent's team—and when you see one, aim several of your heaviest shots through that position.

Pound the Weak Side

Now, let me give you a little sample of how serious this game can be for both offense and defense.

If you've watched a championship prize fight, you've seen a fighter draw blood on his opponent and then continue to pound and punch on that injury. Perhaps you were appalled, but then you weren't in the ring. If you see or hear of a weakness in your competition, be it physical or psychological, work on it. Friend, don't feel guilty, because if the shoe was on the other foot, you'd be blind.

I am not saying that you should hurt anyone physically. In fact, it is seldom that a goal seeker ever gets into real physical contact, though I have on two occasions in the business world had an opponent come after me with his fists, and still another—a woman!—threaten me with a gun. In both cases, reason won out, though I was prepared for the worst.

You will have your share of threats, I'm sure, especially if you are a constant winner. In a fight, somebody almost always gets hurt.

How Do You Make Out a Game Plan?

Begin by having a discussion with your scouting staff to find out the weaknesses, strengths, and security precautions of the opposing roster. Anticipate the favorite defense they will use against you and know who their key defensive players are. Use your imagination: if it's a sales goal you're seeking, for example, objections or objecting players may be the defense.

Now, on a large sheet of paper which has a goal post drawn in the top center, write in your goal. Below this write the names of the persons you can expect to be trying to prevent you from getting to the goal. Alongside their names note the situations in which you expect them to operate. Next, write down the opposition's lesser echelon of players. It will resemble an organization chart and will give you a pretty good picture of the defense. Now you can see who has to be moved out of the way first to open a hole so you can run. Mark which of your players will take out which of the opposing players, in which direction, and with what technique. We will discuss techniques later.

That's a game plan—and it will work if you just plan and play for the first downs and forget about the "long bombs."

Don't Waste Your Time Studying Weaknesses or Losses, Yours or Others

There are so many popular, positive slogans on the subject of success—winning, overcoming, striving—that I could probably fill an entire book with them. But you already know most of them. Most such slogans are quotes from people who were inspired to go the whole nine yards, people like yourself who were not satisfied to be just another Coke bottle—which means a million just alike. I cannot think of one goal seeker I have met who doesn't have a collection of success-inspiring books in his or her library. Achievers use such books as guides and references in designing their game plans. I don't expect that this book is your first crack at exploring the techniques of self-energization, nor should it be your last. If you want to continually be a part of the winning way, you must constantly study the methods and philosophies of proven winners. Your public library has hundreds of self-improvement books and I hope that you, like me and all the other goal seekers I know, have a book handy for those spare moments when you relax between goals. You never can tell when you might just discover the "x factor" for your ultimate goal hidden among the words of another winner.

Keep Track of the Action

Some of you probably feel that I am making too much out of keeping track, because your team members are mature, educated, professional people who know their stuff. But since both you and your team will have a variety of things going at the same time, you'll need a system for checking up. People forget, have accidents, get sick, even go crazy.

I suggest that you keep a checklist of your goals and mark down the progress you are making toward them at regular intervals. Whether this is daily, weekly, or monthly depends on your game plan. I have played for goal seekers who had me call their telephone answering machine and report each day. I use a metal board with magnetic strips that I can write on and place anywhere on the board. Call it a game board if you will. On those movable strips, I record the names and key data about all players on both sides of the game. Visualization in this or any other form is valuable. It lets you *see* what you're thinking—and make revisions if they appear needed.

Genghis Khan was a Sociologist

Old Khan was one hell of a goal seeker—started when he was only thirteen. If you have ever read about the conquest of Genghis Khan you will remember that all of the needs of his warriors were taken care of while the conquest was on and all the bounty went into the general fund. After the battle, the crew's share was equally distributed while the chiefs received a greater share.

Now, as a member of Mr. Khan's team, what do you think you could learn from that?

You would learn that on Mr. Khan's team, you were not automatically promoted. If you lived, you had to request more responsibility in order to increase your share of the bounty. But, there was a catch. You were totally responsible for the welfare and action of your men. If you screwed up and got them injured or killed, you probably wound up dead, too.

By the same token, if you are playing for a goal seeker and you screw up a deal through stupidity and a goal is lost, you lose your share. Odds are that you won't be asked to play again, and some people will be too skeptical to play for you.

The moral is: Give critical responsibilities only to those who want them and who will understand the consequences if they fail through negligence.

Don't Count on Luck

Luck is being in the right place at the right time, recognizing an opportunity and then taking advantage of it.

The best way to be in the right place at the right time is to *plan* on being there—to *know* the time and place in advance—but sometimes you're going to experience plain dumb luck. In that case, the trick is to recognize the right place and time when you stumble into it.

But don't build a luck factor into your game plan. Just be ready to take it if it comes. As a "factor," luck really doesn't exist. A successful gambler is one who plays only the odds that are in his favor. For instance, a good crapshooter knows that a pair of dice can only do thirty-six things, and of those thirty-six combinations, seven will come up the most, six or eight the second most. So, he takes a calculated risk and works with those three numbers. There is an element of *chance* in the professional's dice game, but luck? Never!

Again, your game plan must be based on reliable information and implemented with positive action taken against objectives which you know will exist in a given place at a given time.

It's Not a Life-or-Death Game

Have I made goal seeking sound like a struggle for earthly survival? Forgive me if I've made you think that all goal seekers have ice water for blood and hearts of stone, or that they are incurable workaholics. That would not be a fair description of a typical goal seeker.

I don't know a single successful goal seeker who is not a high energy, outgoing personality who takes charge. Goal seekers are usually dedicated family people. But it's also true that when it comes to business and a career, the goal seeker is a leader, a Class "A" competitor and invariably more intense than the average Joe.

For the most part, a goal seeker is an optimist, outwardly conservative, who may be counted on to point out a positive approach to almost any problem. Still, I won't deny that the goal seeker has a split personality. It splits like an atom when he gets into the game and explodes into victory.

Isn't that too Bad?

Whenever something rotten happens to someone we know, our first reaction is to say, "Isn't that too bad?" In most cases we mean it; but *how* do we mean it? Are we really sorry or just relieved it hasn't happened to us? If you think I'm being absurd or cruel, think about it. I had this situation presented to me as a police officer.

During a raid on a shooting gallery (a place used by addicts to shoot heroin into their own veins) an officer was thrown down an elevator shaft. While the poor guy was in the hospital, we were sitting around in the squad room when one of our men said, "Isn't that too bad?"

A crusty (but good) old sergeant spoke up, saying, "Hell, no! I'm glad!" Well you can imagine the quiet that set in. Then Sarge went on to say, "I'm glad it was him and not me." He had a point because there was no one in that room who would have wanted to be in the injured officer's place.

The lesson is that if you are not properly informed by your scouts of where the open elevator shafts and other hazards are in any game, somebody's going to say, "Isn't it too bad?" about you, and really mean, "I'm glad it wasn't me."

If you've got ideas about where there might be problems in your company, don't be afraid to let your hair down to the boss and tell him what you think can be done to correct them. Or suppose you stumble onto something underhanded like an accounting scam. Do the right thing—speak up—or you're gone and the others will be sorry for you and glad it's not them.

It really *is* too bad for the whole team when poor planning puts a good man out. Check and recheck, scout and rescout every part of your game before you start—and if you're still not sure, ask questions. Some people say they are embarrassed to ask a lot of questions. What the hell? You'll never sound dumb *asking* questions. The only people who look dumb are the ones who can't answer the questions!

Don't Judge Other People for Other People Unless You are Elected to the Bench

Here's a simple bit of advice that may be the most profound I will give you: Don't ever forget the old saying, "If you can't say something good about a person, don't say anything." In other words, keep your opinions about someone who is not directly related to your goal to yourself. I was once asked by an acquaintance (I didn't know the difference between the meaning of friend and acquaintance at the time) to rate a list of persons who were being considered for a very important and highly paid position because I had worked with all of the names on the list. I was flattered by the invitation. At the time I was not seeking a goal that had anything to do with this situation and there was no way I would benefit or lose (I thought). I was also asked to make commitments about the abilities or shortcoming of the individuals listed. To make a long story short, you guessed it, the list and my comments became public knowledge. I hurt the chances of a man who had never done me wrong and I gained nothing. This man has gone on to become a very important and highly successful businessman who has direct influence in an area in which I am constantly involved. I am ashamed of that stupid mistake. Never, never again, will I judge another person who does not directly relate to my personal health, happiness or success. Don't *you* forget it!

There is Enough Room in this World for Everyone to be Successful

If you are one of those people who believe that for every successful person there has to be a failure, one rich for one poor, a life for a death, a beauty for a beast—then, my friend, you are sadly mistaken! Nowhere in the good book does it state that God set quotas. If you believe in Him and live by His Ten Commandments and the Golden Rule, then "ask and ye shall receive."

I guess the first thing you must determine is what you consider success. Next, you must stop thinking of success as intangible—it is something you can feel, see or wear! Success is the second most tangible thing in your life after *love.* You bet your bippy—you can *feel, see* and *wear* love and success—and they both will outshine the brightest jewelry, make you more attractive and desirable than the most fashionable apparel. Success and love walk hand in hand, and to be the one—successful—you must practice the other—love.

You must love yourself. That's not being conceited or narcissistic, it merely means that you have a heap of confidence in all that you are, and are sincere in all that you do.

Degrees of success are judged only in the eyes of the one who succeeds, that's you.

The amazing Grace Smith, the captain of most all of my goal seeking teams, commented recently when we heard that an acquaintance of ours who had just taken two steps by himself after a severe and paralyzing stroke—"Now that's success." Two steps might not be a big deal to you and me, but if someone told you that you would never walk again, and you put time, effort, blood, sweat and tears into the effort to walk two steps—you would think it was a bigger accomplishment than a gold medal in the Olympics.

Your goals can and should bring you health, wealth, peace of mind, happiness and total fulfillment.

The first step into a world full of successful people is easy—It's called the *Golden Rule.* The second step is—set a *goal.*

Never, Never be Satisfied to Just be One of the Crowd

I repeat this because it is so important that you never accept the idea that you are just average, one of the crowd, part of the mass, one of the silent majority, one of the crew, a follower, part of a flock or any other tag that implies that you don't have the imagination as well as the get up and go to be "El Hombre"—*the man!*

No, I am not saying in the moral sense of the word that you are better than anyone else; you are, however, different from any other member of any group.

As a goal seeker, you have sincere wants for a better, fuller, happier, more creative and financially rewarding life for you and your family. And unless you break out of the pack like a race car driver, you can't win. So, never let any person, persons or situation box you into the crowd.

After Goal Seeking Comes Goal Tending

It is not enough to want a goal and work to attain it. You and your team must be capable of maintaining and building the goal after you have won. A big part of a well designed game plan is the maintenance team. This team should be as carefully selected as the acquisition team. It would be a darn shame if everything you fought for fell apart after you acquired it because no one knew how to keep it healthy and growing. One of the biggest mistakes I have observed in the current crop of management moguls is their urge to fix a newly acquired toy, when it isn't broken. They seem to feel it's necessary to put their mark of authority on an acquisition to insure its loyalty. Unless you are attaining a goal solely for its assets and intend to dispose of the property, and equipment, then I highly recommend reaching an immediate understanding that present management (if it is competent and the business is healthy) will continue. Put a member of your team into place as a counselor and make no changes for ninety days.

Part II
Second Quarter

Chapter 5

A Good Team Is Always Up for the Game

Your team could have the best collection of talent in the country, but if one or more players aren't in the mood to participate, you've got a problem. It doesn't matter whether the man is a fullback with a pigskin tucked under his arm or an advertising creative director with a campaign theme for a product tucked away in his brain. Both have to move through a maze of persons or obstacles bent on stopping them. To score, each must be at peak performance.

Players have to be in condition. They also have to be in the *mood*. In that respect, the game of business is a lot like sex.

It's your goal that is at stake, so make sure nobody's asleep on the field.

If you have employed people and had them quit on you, you know that most people stop working long before they ever come in and say "I quit." The goal seeker soon learns to look for the signs of letdown. He controls the hiring and firing of his players and he never waits for a formal resignation.

Don't Make Promises You Can't or Don't Intend to Keep

When you have decided on a goal, set a budget and timetable, scouted the competition and started to recruit a team, make darn sure you'll be able to honor any offer you make a player.

Never go back on an offer. If you do, the word will soon go out and you will find that no one will play for you. Promises get a lot of would-be goal seekers into trouble, because from the time a promise is made until it's time to call it in, many circumstances can change.

It's a good idea to keep a written record of your promises, just as if they were monetary debts, and try to get them all paid off as soon as possible. A promise is a promise and you are morally obligated to honor it, no matter what.

Make Sure You Select the Best Pros Around

I learned this the hard way and it cost me a great deal of money, not to mention some human-relations losses and a residue of hard feelings that were not easy to get over.

My mistake was picking an attorney as a team member for one of my goals because he had a well-known name. He was a hell of a criminal lawyer but he had little business experience. I guess I fell for his publicity. A rule to remember is that good press or a famous name does not necessarily make a person a pro. Some of the biggest names in headlines are not pros, and don't you forget it.

Some of my best players have been quiet, unassuming individuals who never had a reputation for anything—except results.

Pick the players who *play* good rather than just *look* good.

A Pat on the Back Does Wonders for Morale

I was sitting in the office of the president of a major American corporation. He had agreed to give me a complete profile of the company and its officers, which I needed for—you guessed it—a scouting report. He telephoned the man who was in charge of the communications department and told him to bring in the corporate annual report and some other financial data. When he did so, the president took the documents and dismissed him with no more than a mumbled "thank you."

As the man left the room, I could see disappointment in his eyes. I looked through the report and damned near fell off my chair. It was probably the finest example of its kind I'd ever seen. Obviously, a lot of hard work had gone into that document.

I told the president what a fine job the man had done, in my opinion. His reply was a shocker. He said, "Hell, why not? That's what I pay him for."

Expert reporters, report writers and analysts are rare, and that boss should have shown the same appreciation of the man's work that I did. I showed mine in a different way. I got the name of the writer, invited him to lunch, and sincerely complimented him on the work he had done. That pat on the back paid off. The man was soon to retire from that company and today he is one of my chief scouts.

Give praise where it's deserved and you'll get what you deserve in loyalty, plus that little extra it takes for the team to win. But always praise with sincerity. A phony compliment is worse than none at all. It is probably the worst form of lying.

Don't Criticize without Giving Suggestions for Improvement

If you have a complaint about a player's performance, first discuss it with that player—in private. Second, be ready with a suggestion on how the player can correct or improve his performance. Otherwise keep your mouth shut.

You should also keep your mouth shut if something a player is doing is interfering with the rest of the team. Just be patient and let nature take its course. The other members of the team will provide all the criticism the erring player needs.

Of course, if the player making the booboos won't listen to criticism from anybody, get a substitute fast.

No Team-Wide Penalties

I once knew a man who took a Christmas bonus away from a whole department because the department showed a loss. Instead of doing some research to find the causes of the loss, he just arbitrarily punished everyone. The staff knew why the loss occurred and who was guilty. The manager later learned the facts, but by then it was too late for him. Within sixty days, old Scrooge had lost every employee in that department to competing firms. Within ninety days he himself was out of a job.

Punishment is an individual thing. They only send the guilty man to jail, not his whole family. So, don't lose your temper and fine the entire team. Remember, too, that snap judgments applied to a group will snap back at you not once, but as many times as there are people in that group.

Also, make a note that you can *never* honestly criticize players if you change an agreement in the middle of a game and find it is not followed. Stick with your plan or your players will tell you where to stick it.

Make Sure Your Players Understand the Plays

This sounds simple enough. Everybody knows that practice makes perfect, yet at the end of each football season the networks compile a whole hour or so of famous flubs that happened during crucial moments of professional football games. I mean these foul-ups happened to guys who practice until they are blue in the face. You see these characters running into each other or, for the biggest laughs of the season, running the wrong way.

Well, my goal seeking friend, just wait until some members of your team show up at the wrong time and the wrong location—you won't think it's funny when it's your nose that's in the mud.

In goal seeking, you will use razzle-dazzle plays on a regular basis and there are far more plays in life and business than there are in football. It is absolutely necessary that everyone on your team knows where and when to move. I can't stress this point enough. It doesn't matter whether it's business or police work, you must be aware of *what* the other players are going to do and *when.*

Back in my police days, my partners on vice and narcotics took me into some pretty tough situations. The plays we devised were more often tricky and had to be on the numbers. We practiced every move until we could do it in our sleep, and then we practiced again to be sure. Now, granted, when you're only playing for money or position as an objective, the most you can lose is money, or you may lose face. If things go wrong, you can play another day. However, when I was on the police force, we might have to run a play through three doors, a window and a garage door all at the same time, and what we had to lose was our lives! We had to know who was going to shoot, when, and in what direction. Friendly bullets kill you just as dead as those fired by criminals. Everyone in police work has to understand the play.

I said before that military training is good background for a goal seeker. So is police work. As with soldiers in battle, it forces you to seek your goals as if your life depended on it—because it does.

Assume, as I do to this day, that your life is at stake in every game. Get your players thinking the same way. You'll shape up fast!

No Room for Free-Loaders

I have told you not to select second-stringers. I've warned you about running a taxi squad, and here I am alerting you to the hazards of free-loaders. What the hell? Isn't there *anyone* you can rely on?

Of course, there are persons you can depend on, but right now I want to put you wise to the player who just puts out what is asked of him or her, nothing more and nothing less. I think what I'm looking for is called *Esprit de Corps,* the common spirit. Can you stand another war story from my police experience?

On the vice detail there was one team assigned to check the Class C establishments (bars) to see that the licenses were up to date and no drunks, hookers or other undesirables were on the premises. It was a task most officers didn't like. For one thing, it required more drinking than most officers consider safe. Drinking on duty can kill a cop—and I don't mean what it does to the liver. That wipes out a little myth, doesn't it? Anyway, there was this one guy on the squad who seemed to do his job well enough. He was willing to volunteer for this unpopular duty and he was neat about typing up his reports and all that, but when he was out in the patrol car, he never did more than the bare minimum. If we had to make an emergency back-up run on another car in the territory—covering the men in that other car for their safety—this bare-minimum buddy wouldn't even get out of the car. Once, in a tight spot an officer got hurt while ole bare-minimum buddy stayed in the car. If that permanent passenger had been out where he belonged, his partner wouldn't have been hurt.

I had a short talk with that strange fellow and discovered his problem. He was scared to play. He was afraid of getting hurt in the action. Indeed, he was free-loading on our lives!

Anybody who goes along for the ride is a free-loader. Invite all such individuals to "take a walk."

Don't Run Your Team Ragged

In goal seeking you are not always required to play every day. The reason is evident. Opportunities for advancement toward your goal simply don't present themselves every day. Some games take weeks, months, even years to play out, and that, incidentally, is why you generally have more than one game at a time in progress—and some that are more urgent and important than others. If a play is not absolutely essential or won't pick up any yardage, don't keep sending your players out for passes just to keep the arm in shape. If you do, they will soon get bored and possibly even ask to get out of their contract.

Meetings that are not necessary and phone calls that don't really accomplish anything all fall into this category. You can overdo "fire drills" to the point that everybody's too tired to answer the bell when a real fire breaks out.

Enforce Curfews

It sounds kind of childish, doesn't it? Grown men and women have to have bed check. Silly as it sounds, it's true. I hear pro athletic team members bitch about it all the time, but they comply. If they don't, they get penalized.

As a goal seeker, of course, nobody's going to spank you and put you to bed. The curfew has to be self-imposed. If you have an important meeting in connection with a goal, then for the sake of the game, get yourself rested and prepared. Make sure none of your other players are out helling around the night before a big contest. Too many fumbles and turnovers *start* the night before.

Never Call a Play You Wouldn't Run Yourself

If you're in a tough game and find that you have to use some particular player a great deal, consider the value of the player as well as the yardage you're after. If you can see the player's tail is dragging, take another look at your play list and run some "clock-stoppers" to the sidelines until you can get your star some rest. A "clock-stopper" in business is simply taking a day off. Make it two, if time is not critical.

Don't you dare run a player any longer or harder than you would be willing to run yourself. A tired player is a weak player. You'll not only lose the ball—you'll lose the player.

Chapter 6

Understanding the Rules

There are rules for everything—and everybody. In the introduction of this book I said that I had arrested pimps, con-men, prostitutes and thieves with more moral fiber than some of the business people I've had to deal with in later years.

Seldom will you find a street person who does an act out of pure viciousness. They may steal to eat and kill to survive, but unadulterated viciousness for no apparent reason is something I have run into more often with so-called "straight" people.

When you work the streets, your life depends on doing the right thing at the right time. You play by the rules of the street or you are dead. There is a set of unwritten but nevertheless strict rules by which the street people play. Though these rules are rough, they are fair. They are fair because they relate to the results their makers are attempting to attain. For example, I once laid tin (identified myself as a police officer and showed my badge) in a drug deal I'd participated in, and my backup man was a minute or two late. I had my back exposed to a doorway, and suddenly I heard a warning from behind me. I whirled around and, at the same instant, my backup arrived and got the drop on the man who had warned me—he could have shot me in the back, and he had reason to: he was a three-time loser who would get a life sentence as a habitual criminal if he was caught. But back-shooting was not his way of life, and that saved mine. The answer is no, I didn't arrest him. He was killed three weeks later, though—shot in the back!

In the business world you will discover games that are played with no rules, written or unwritten. Anything goes. I have seen men's careers murdered for no reason at all. The weapons have been character defamation, lying, stealing and entrapment to name a few, and they have been employed out of pure wanton viciousness. So, watch out for rattlesnakes and learn to set your own rules and live or lose by them.

If you're in doubt about what kind of rules, there's always a good sample to work from. It's called the Golden Rule. Do unto others as you would have them do unto you.

Who Sets the Rules?

I'll answer that with another question, "What is a rule?" No, I'm not trying to confuse you, but I do want you to think read, research, ask questions, listen and discuss. Let's go to the universal source of simple explanations, the dictionary:

> **rule** (1) a guide or principle for governing action (2) the usual way of doing something

Let's dispose of the second definition first. The usual way of doing something is a habit and habits belong to people, to you, that is. As to the main definition, if the action is yours, then the guide or principle is yours, too. So, who makes the rules? You do! Yes, my bright, creative, aggressive, goal-seeking friend, you make up the rules by which you will live, play, and in some cases, die.

I once worked with an officer who made it a rule never to draw a weapon unless he intended to use it, an excellent rule and one every good officer should know. This officer, Gus, was with us when we flushed out a couple of Murphy Men, guys who wait in ambush while an accomplice brings in a "John" (sucker) to some location where a prostitute is supposed to be. Then they rob and beat him and in many instances kill him. Before it was "get down time," we had worked out our game plan and knew our assigned duties. There were three of us flushing and we had a bird dog posing as a John. Our bird dog would let himself be guided to the Murphy Men and then we'd nail them.

Everything worked until one of the Murphs drew a gun and headed into a vacant building. I yelled to Gus that the man was armed, but Gus said, "I didn't see a gun" and went into that building without his weapon in his hand. The Murphy Men made their move before the rest of us could get in the building. Gus . . . he had a rule and he died by it.

Give a lot of thought to the rules you make—or take—to play by. You may think you can change a rule in the middle of the game, but it's not that easy. Once rules become habits, they're going to *rule you.* So, try hard to find the rules that have the least possible exceptions.

Points to Consider when Setting the Rules

You know what? I wish I hadn't put myself in such a box! Here I am in the position of having to help guide you in setting up rules, but since I'm the guy who got you this far, I'm duty bound to give you some insight into what is probably the most difficult part of the goal seeker's game.

As I said, there is a big difference between "street people" and Dun & Bradstreet people. Everybody sees good and evil in different ways. I myself am a great (note I didn't say firm) believer in non-conformity when it comes to what most people call ethics, and I recognize an important difference between the concepts of rules and laws.

I therefore conform only to the law of the tribe and the Ten Commandments. If you develop your rules with these in mind, you can be a winner and well-respected as well. No rules are easier to remember or more comfortable to play by.

Make the Rules Loud and Clear

When you have finally decided on the rules, make sure that you spell them out in the simplest possible language and that everyone playing on your team fully understands them. If a player is uncomfortable with even one of the rules, make a player substitution on the spot. Remember, we are talking about your future and the future is a long, long time.

What About the Other Team's Rules?

What about them? Oh! You think they are going to play the same kind of game you do when it comes to values? Don't be stupid. They sure as hell aren't going to do it. They may play fair or they may play dirty, but even if they play fair, their rules won't be exactly the same as yours.

I have played some of my toughest, roughest games in business against some super straight shooters. We both had some minor penalties, but that can't be helped. At least with the straight shooters we never had to worry about getting our heads knocked off or our backs broken. On the other hand, I've been in games with teams that started out by stealing the referee's flipping coin and then went downhill from there. I have to tell you that I don't mind putting the old big ten on those slobs. The best approach is to play it straight and play it tight. A win feels a thousand times greater when you can face yourself in the locker room mirror and smile, though you may look funny with a missing tooth and a busted nose.

Penalties Can Cost You a Game

I'll bet you're fit to be tied now. Right? You can't figure out, if both sides make the rules by which they play, how in the hell you can be penalized, or by whom?

There is a ringer in our goals seeker's game. She is the lady with the blindfold and scale that decorates your local courthouse steps and provides a roost for the pigeons—Ma Justice. Just when you think you have a first down after some razzle-dazzle play, one of the pigeons flies out to drop his "flag" on you. It's just a thing that pigeons do, and you can't fight it at the moment.

Pigeons? Justice? Huh? Here's the point. I consider an attorney a *running back,* and if you can find one who really wants to play, you've got a winner. Remember what I said about rules and laws? The attorney minds the store where laws are concerned.

You don't have to be guilty of anything to get slapped with a lawsuit these days, so put a lawyer into play and keep those pigeons away.

No Arguing with the Referee

The way we goal seekers play, any discussions that take place on the field just waste time. The referee in this case is a plural one—the courts and the judges. Avoid them at all cost. It's time-consuming and cash-consuming. Of course, if you really think you're getting too much pressure from the opposition and lousy officiating and your running back, the attorney, wants to go into league headquarters and the commissioner, go ahead and do it. Good luck!

Don't Ever Make a Threat, Only a Promise

If you are anxious to play this game of success and rewards, then there will come times in your playing career when you will be faced with situations that can get physical as well as vocal—and in some very public places and at most inopportune times.

Since most of the folks you will be playing against inhabit the same clubs, shops and restaurants that you do, and since you are sure to have a few things in common, you are bound to have a confrontation from time to time—especially when the other team captain finds out you are after his job or his company, land, or assets.

Here's what you do in a confrontation or shouting match. Let the other side talk, and loudly. The louder they yell and the politer you listen, the better you'll appear—especially if it's a public place and there are ladies present. That's yardage for you. You may even find yourself accepting the opponent's apologies. Maybe you'd rather not, but accept them gracefully, at least for the moment. Then, when you can get that opponent in private, face down old Big Mouth and inform him in a courteous, straightforward way that if he ever does that again, you will bust his business balls. This should not be a threat, but a promise!

Once when I was under cover as a cop and it came time to lay tin, I shouted to a felon in a restaurant, "I am a police officer and you are under arrest. Don't make any sudden moves or I'll blow your head off. I mean that for everybody!"

This was no idle threat. It was a promise. Nobody moved. The mayor, eating at a table next to the felon's, didn't care much for my style, but when he learned that the criminal was armed, he complimented me as an especially "promising" member of the force.

Chapter 7

The Risk Factor

We are all aware that there is a certain amount of risk in everything we do—from walking down a flight of stairs to crossing the street or eating in a new restaurant. People ordinarily take all of these risk factors in stride, without giving them a second thought. A goal seeker must accept much larger risk factors in exactly the same way.

It won't take a good sincere goal seeker long to be able to size up a situation and make a decision, using a built-in risk-factor gauge—instinct. Learn how to trust your hunches and measure risks automatically. When you get a "feeling" something is wrong, always heed your feeling. It's better to be safe than sorry—check it out!

The word *risk* has a terrible reputation, thanks to stockbrokers and bankers. One talks you into taking risks while the other keeps trying to talk you out.

Some people even try to disguise the word by calling it an "occupational hazard," all of which boils down to the same thing—taking a chance. You can usually take a chance if you know what it is you're taking. Otherwise the chance takes you!

When Gunning for a Win,
Walk in and Take Careful Aim

I am not what you would call a typical reader. As a matter of fact, I will more often than not have as many as four books going all at the same time and they may be as assorted in content as a bag of Christmas candy. They could include a mystery, a historical novel, a western, medical book, biography or autobiography. Now, for some folks it could get confusing, but for me it's no problem to pick up wherever I left off in any particular book. My retention is not lost. That's because I pay keen attention. In almost every book there is some information or stimulation that helps me toward one or more of my goals.

However, I'm getting away from my point a little. It's the western fiction and nonfiction I want to talk about. There's a lot of romance about the old gunfighters of the pioneer West. They always stressed accuracy as well as speed. They have impressed me with the importance of knowing where my shots are going, not where I hope they're going.

Whenever I have a new goal seeker come to me after losing in a shoot-out at the K.O. Corral (that's K.O. as in Knock-Out), that person asks me what went wrong. The first thing I look at is the scouting reports. How many guns were waiting for him? Did he know the enemy's reputation for speed and accuracy with weapons? And, what kind of weapons? Usually, the story I get is that "we were outgunned." That's usually because the man accepted his scouts' reports as gospel, not taking into consideration that the defense had increased its number of guns since the last report.

The lesson is: don't make up the game plan without taking into consideration possible last-minute changes by the other team. Go in slow, test the defenses, note the numbers and observe the shooting skills. Then take careful aim and let fly.

Sure you're going to get your lumps now and then, but that's not a risk, just an "occupational hazard."

Calculated Risks are a Must

I can own, manage, and quarterback a team in a goal seeker's game, but I'd really make a lousy football coach. How come? Aren't the two games played in a similar manner? The key word here is "similar" not meaning same.

To begin with, football coaches in high schools, colleges and to some extent professional ball all have one thing in common. They're in it because they love the game. Sure they want to win, because that's the only way they can keep their jobs and keep on playing. To that degree, their outlook resembles that of the goal seeker.

Where we differ is that *our* game is not designed in a way that would even consider letting the defense get its hands on the ball—and there are two players that are never in our line-up. There are no kickers and punters. We don't go for three points or kick the ball away in a tight situation and hope we get another shot at it.

The goal seeker must take the calculated risk of running or passing on the fourth down every time, and with every intention of completing it. Sure we have turnovers, but they are always by accident, never calculated. There's no offside or margin for error in the goal seeker's game!

Stupid Chances are a No-no

For those of you who are jumping up and down in frustration because I just said, "We shoot the works on the fourth down," and saying, "If that ain't stupid, what is?"—sit down and relax while I attempt to make it sound logical.

If you have comprehended what I've been saying thus far, then you already realize why we must take the chances we take. We're not in a spectator sport and our revenues come only from the pot between the goal posts, not from the box office or hotdog concession. Since our only reward is achieving our goals, we must use every down to gain yardage and take care not to lose the ball on a turnover. In business, if you're not gaining, you're losing.

The biggest and most stupid chance you can take in my opinion is using inexperienced players in situations that you know are over their heads. Another big one is using the same play over and over with no ground gained. Sometimes that is also an indication that the goal is not realistic, that you have somehow confused a dream with a goal. No play you could ever call would make a dream come true.

Make sure you're never dreaming when you're supposed to be planning. That could be taking the biggest chance you ever dreamed of.

No Room for Show-offs or Prima Donnas

If you get opposition from one of your players, watch out! I'm talking about your own player who may want to dominate the game or take the quarterback position from you. If you find such a player on your team, then suggest that he go set his own goal and form his own team. Pay him off and let him go. As a further precaution, keep your eyes on the defense. You may just have to change your game plan because your old hot jock is peddling his services to the other side after you cut him loose.

We always want to remember that in our game of goal seeking, we're all playing for pieces of gold and the player we lay off can get the same gold pieces or even more from the other team.

Don't feel so bad if you have to release a player. If he shows up on the enemy side, well, you already know his style and his limitations, so maybe it's not a loss at all but a big gain!

What Do You Really Have to Lose?

To answer this question, you have to consider the type of goal. Is it personal, career, or financial in nature? The one thing you lose in all of them is the most important thing of all: time.

In pursuing a financial goal, you may lose money. But money can always be recovered, no matter how much it is, if you are any kind of a goal seeker.

In seeking personal goals, a failure can cost you some self-confidence but all you need is a re-charge and you get that back again, free.

It's in the quest of those long-term career goals, that you face the biggest risk, because so many careers are based on an age factor. *Time* is the biggest possible loss in any goal seeker's game, but it's a most serious loss along the career line. Time is precious. Time is life.

A Win Makes It Worth It

There are different degrees of glory in a win—depending on how long and tough the game was and the number of injuries your team sustained.

Before evaluating a win, you will want to subtract any damage your reputation may have suffered in the particular league in which you were contending. Oh, sure! The team that lost is going to comment on the quality of your play. They won't fault you for being rough and tough, but they'll never forgive you for a foul, whether real or imagined.

Of course, if you get a reputation for winning, whatever they try to do to the rest of your reputation can't hurt you much. So, weigh all of the factors and *smile* when you win . . . and remember what I said about giving thanks and credit where due.

Power Goals Are Never Permanent

That heading just about says it all. However, I feel compelled to explain why you must avoid at all cost working toward a goal for which the only reward is power over others. It won't last.

Sooner or later a person who is *power struck* is going to stumble and fall—with the glide angle of a brick.

Whenever I encounter power addicts, I am tempted to recommend that they see an Optocolonaligist and have him fit them with a plexiglass bellybutton. They need one to see where they are going, because their anatomy is misadjusted—they have their head in the wrong place.

Being power struck is a direct result of paranoia and usually indicates massive insecurity or an urge to take vengeance. Those kinds of goals are doomed to destruction, one way or another.

Criticism is Really a Compliment in Disguise

I'll bet that statement raises an eyebrow or two. You cannot successfully pursue success without picking up a whole string of critics.

The trick to accepting criticism and using it to your advantage is in realizing that criticism is an indication of weakness and jealousy and points to what probably is a guilt complex. Critics may feel that your accomplishments and success should be theirs. But their failure to persistently pursue a goal as you did is a personal failure on their part. Any action they can take to reduce your esteem, will divert any attention from their own failures.

Just *try*, try real hard to remember that the degree of your success is in direct proportion to the quality of your critics, how successful and well-known they are in the field.

Part III
Third Quarter

Chapter 8

Game Time

It's the moment of truth. If you have taken all the advice I have offered, if you have fitted it to your own style, if you have set a realistic goal and scouted the defenses, then you're ready to leave the locker room.

However, before you go onto the field, make sure there is no unexpected opposition such as General Custer had to face. Make certain you have the best selection of players available and that both you and your players are sure of the game plan and are comfortable with it.

You're confident that your team is ready to play and understands all of your rules, right? O.K. You're ready for the kick-off. The test of a team is not how it looks in practice but how it performs under pressure, how it reacts to changing situations.

Never forget that the goal seeker's game is one in which you must keep the *offensive* advantage. There are few, if any, defensive plays in this game. Once you're called for a violation and must go to a defensive style of play, you're in deep trouble.

Play as hard as you can. Use every strategy that will accomplish your objective as quickly and safely as possible. This is what you have decided to do and now the game is on for real.

Never Hold a Grudge, but
Don't Forget the Bastard

As we were growing up, we were constantly reminded to forgive and forget, kiss and make up, and to turn the other cheek. All these sayings are well and good when it comes to family matters, perhaps, although I have seen reason to question that other old saying, the one that goes: "blood is thicker than water."

In the goal seekers' society, if you were to attempt to live by and practice these philosophies, you could get your head handed to you on a plate. If a guy does you dirty, you might show him another cheek, but never turn your head so far you haven't got an eye on the S.O.B. You might forgive a foul-maker in your heart, but you're in trouble if you ever *forget* what he did to you.

You can avoid the whole problem of forgiving, of course, by avoiding any associations with con artists in the first place. Don't recruit them for your team and don't play for them.

If you get stiffed on a deal or by a player on your own squad or one on any team you may play for, then remember, don't ever give that individual another shot at you. I don't say this vindictively either. Don't waste any of your precious time and effort on getting even. Sooner or later your paths will cross and it's what you do or don't do at that time that will eventually settle that old score—and you won't need to waste any time or compromise any of your rules either. My Grandma Putt had an old but wise saying on that subject that is so good, I'm making it the heading of the next section:

The Wheel of Vengeance Rolls
over Him Who Starts It

A good proof of the truth of my Grandma's saying is found in the history of Genghis Khan. In about the year 1216, Genghis had just removed a thorn of many years from his side—a Naiman chief by the name of Kushlek—in a battle on the Khuarezm Frontier, in territory ruled by one Shah Muhammed.

Genghis then decided he did not want to fight anymore, or push farther into Moslem territory. He hung up the scimitar and sent envoys to Muhammed with presents and a friendly message asking for peace and trade privileges. The Shah said he'd be pleased, so Genghis sent a party over to trade. However, one Inaljuk, a governor for the Shah, didn't like the idea and put the peaceful missionaries to death. Genghis Khan demanded extradition of Inaljuk, but Shah Muhammed refused. Adding insult to injury, the Shah had a couple of Genghis Khan's messengers killed and shaved the beards of others and sent them back. The rest is history. Genghis Khan took everything Shah Muhammed owned. The moral is: if you mess with the bull, you get the horn.

Better to Lose the Game than Lose Your Temper

I have seen and heard people do some of the damndest things when they are mad, and on more than one occasion I have provoked a person into getting mad because I stood to gain from it.

For example, there was a big, well dressed, diamond studded narcotics dealer who I was certain was holding a sample or two. I also have to tell you that he limped and wore those large, built-up shoes made for people with one leg shorter than the other. Every evening he would hang out in a certain bar with all his gold and glitter sparkling, and he'd go in and out to talk to folks in cars that stopped in front of the place.

Well, right there near the door of that joint was a sewer, and during the day my partner and I dressed up like DPW (Department of Public Works) guys, removed the sewer grate and played in the mud. Before leaving, we draped a sheet of black plastic under the sewer cover to catch anything that might drop through the holes in the grate.

That night we did a light roust on the location. Jewelry Joe and I had a little talk out front and I went out of my way to say things to get him riled up. I inferred that the jewelry he wore was phony junk and that the only "shit" (heroin) he ever had was pure Domino (white powered sugar). He got mad enough to kill, and before you could wiggle Samantha's nose, he drew a deck of heroin, split it with his finger, dropped the deck through a hole in the sewer cover and then came over and jammed his finger in my mouth. He had thought he had disposed of the evidence and now wanted to show me that he was no small-time pusher. He sure wasn't. What I tasted was heavy, and that meant he was selling to big dealers, not street fixers.

Well, old Joe had lost more than his temper. It was now my privilege to give him a little working over while my partners recovered the medicine from our sewer trap. At one point he tried to run away. That's when I noticed he didn't limp, so when we overtook him, I pulled off his shoes and broke open those built-up soles. You guessed it. He was walking on million-dollar shoes with heels and platforms hollowed out to conceal the "H."

The moral here is *don't let anybody get you mad.* In the dictionary *mad* not only means angry, it means *crazy.* Don't let an antagonist get you acting nuts. Just walk away or clam up.

Friendships Are in Neutral when the Game is On

Have you ever noticed that when pro football teams come out for the pregame warmup, players from opposing teams will shake hands, hug each other or exchange jokes. Once the game starts, however, they block, tackle, pull and push one another as if they are out to kill. Then, as soon as the game is over, they laugh and joke again on the way off the field. The winners accept congratulations and the losers get some ribbing. Do you wonder how this can be?

It's simple. Many have played as teammates in the past and the odds are that they may do so again. Their wives and kids associate with each other. That is how it should be. When the game is on, though, all that counts is what goes on there on the field. When the whistle blows, both sides go out to win the glory and the gold.

You'd better get used to facing friends or former teammates on the opposing side. You like each other and respect one another for your abilities, but when you talk, talk about anything except the upcoming game or the one in progress.

Naturally, you'll play to win, not to kill . . . and when the game's over, sure, discuss it play by play. Of course, if the loser doesn't know how you won, it's not up to you to tell him.

Leave Your Love in the Locker Room

Don't drag your wife, husband, girlfriend or boyfriend along when you have a game-plan assignment. Having non-playing visitors just makes it harder for you to concentrate on the play and your part in its execution. I mean it can cause a game to be lost. If you are married and the woman with you isn't your wife or vice versa, the defense might find a way to exploit that relationship and use it against you. Your team and your game could be in for a lot of trouble and I've seen it happen more times than I care to count.

Granted, your private life is your own business, but when you make it public, it becomes everybody's business. I can give you a specific example that still makes me uncomfortable when I think about it.

I fly some three thousand miles a week, from coast to coast, making appearances, lecturing, filming, attending meetings, etc. One day I was in a small southern city airport when I ran into a gentleman who had been a business opponent of mine for a long time. We'd gone head-to-head a couple of times in competition for large sales of merchandise, and I knew he was a mean, dirty player who had tried to damage the careers of others without reason. It didn't surprise me at all that this turkey was with a lady whose luggage bore initials that didn't match those of his wife.

I said "hello" because I couldn't avoid it and went on my way. I had no intention of causing trouble for the guy by mentioning the meeting to anyone, because I like to win in ways that let me sleep well. I promptly put it out of mind, although it had given me a little more insight into the guy's character. Three days later I was awakened in the middle of the night by a phone call. It was that same old swinger, calling from out of the country to tell me he was pulling his proposal away from a client that both of us were courting. "You can have the sale," he said. "You deserve a big commission. And by the way, old buddy, you haven't seen me in weeks, have you?" I mumbled something vaguely reassuring, I hadn't intended to tell anybody anyhow, and I didn't. I was both glad and mad. And nine months later I was sad—for the guy's wife. She'd found out about his cheating and filed suit for divorce.

Not long after that I got another phone call from that individual. He had a new game going, he said, and he wanted me to team up with him. I think you can guess my answer. Why should I be so foolish? He had an ax to grind and I would be the turkey.

I had better make myself clear on one more point. I am not opposed to wives, husbands and boyfriends, or girlfriends going on business trips. It's your business. But make sure you don't trip over them in the action.

Don't Rest on Your Laurels
from the Last Successful Game

We have all seen undefeated teams go into the stadium on any given Sunday against the 0 for 8 team in the league and get the daylights kicked out of them. Going home bruised, battered and beaten, they wonder what hit them.

To avoid that kind of shock, prepare for every game as if it were for the league championship, no matter how tough or not-so-tough the competition is rated to be. Even if you're certain you'll slaughter them, play to win! You always have the option of holding down the score. There are no secrets to success. One word describes the formula: *work*. Success has no longevity. Unless you continue to *work* maintaining it, success will fade.

Talk It Up

Watch any professional team—football, hockey, baseball, basketball or soccer—and you'll observe all the guys on the sidelines yelling and hollering to the guys in the game. It's called talking it up. It's needless to say that the players out there under the helmets can't hear much, but they know that they are being rooted for and it helps a hell of a lot. In our goal seeker's game, we can call to our fellow players, too, and give them a word of encouragement. Our players, of course, will have no trouble hearing the cheers. We can also consult and advise, so do it—and often. It works!

Talk it up in your huddles and on the sidelines. Talk it up out to the field. The more you communicate encouragement—as well as information—to each other, the easier it is to win.

Never Intentionally Maim the Opposition;
Just Bruise the Hell out of Them!

I heard one of the most disturbing remarks I've ever heard in my life from a college football coach. He made the remark to the father of a player who had been dropped from the team. "The only trouble with your kid, mister," said the coach, "is that he doesn't have the killer instinct." Now, I don't know what the purpose behind this remark was, but I considered it stupid, vile, and inhumane. I think he would have been much closer to the truth if he had simply said, "Your boy just doesn't have the desire to play football."

If a person doesn't have a real desire to do something, no matter what that something is, he will not do it well. This is more true in our game of goal seeking than in any other kind of game. The reason is that you will often be playing alone and against some very tough odds, and if you don't have the deep-down desire to pursue your goal against any odds, you won't play well, and you will lose.

Conversely, if you *have* that real sincere desire to win and get the prize, then the defense has its hands full.

Just don't let the feeling or the word *desire* ever be compared with—or mistaken for—a killer instinct. Play hard and play as fair as you would have others play against you, but don't be deliberately cruel or destructive.

If that coach ever had to play in some of the games my partners and I have played in—games in which the opposing team really *did* have the killer instinct and proved it—I think he would soon lose his own desire.

Now, here's something for critics of goal seeking to think about:

I was involved in a game in which a small business was the intended goal. It was a successful business which had been started by the gentleman who carried the title of president. I say he "carried" the title because he was no longer active in the day-to-day operations, even though he still had an office and, at the age of eighty-one, came in every day for an hour or so. The company was actually owned by his two sons and a son-in-law, to whom the father had sold the company to eliminate any estate hassle.

You get the picture. The family had no real interest in the business and wanted to sell. I heard about it and made an offer, only to find out that some other party was already in the game. I really wanted this company, so I put goether a team: real estate specialist, heavy machinery expert, market researcher, and a labor specialist. They gave me an in-depth report.

Now I was ready for the game with the other prospective buyer, but there was one wrinkle that bothered me. The founder apparently did not know the business was to be sold. His sons and son-in-law had not told him because they felt he would interfere, even though he had no power.

I checked this out personally by asking one of my players, who was also a friend of the father-founder, to arrange a luncheon for me with the old gentleman. At our meeting, it quickly became evident that the old man was totally unaware of the intentions of his family and that he expected the business to be in his name for quite a while to come. I also learned that he had a serious heart condition. This information came from another one of my players. I immediately made a call to a physician I trust and asked him what might happen if the father were told that the company, his life's work, was about to be traded away. The doctor said that the least that could happen would be a serious depression which might weaken the man's will to live and take care of himself. The worst could be that the shock could kill him. I thanked the physician for his opinion and immediatcly withdrew my team.

You see, if a man can go toe-to-toe and nose-to-nose with me, I'm in the game, but if my action in competition will cause any physical or mental harm to an innocent party, then I won't continue—no matter how bad I want that goal, because that's maiming. *Being fair* is what gets your "fair" share!

Go for the Ball

If you are a one-man team in a one-man game of goal seeking, you carry the ball at all times. My advice is: tuck it in tight, and if you're stopped, get the other hand on it fast.

If, on the other hand, you have a team backing you up and someone fumbles the ball, don't just stand there like a bump on a log. Dive on that ball!

Once play has slowed or halted and you're not out there forcing the issues, getting things done, remember that the goal seeker's clock doesn't stop after a play. You will have reports to get, appointments to make. Don't let the ball sit there. Try a play in the other direction. Keep it moving. A delayed game is a bummer.

Chapter 9

Calling the Plays

In a real football game, most of the plays are sent into the quarterback on instructions from the coach on the sidelines. Very few quarterbacks are given the responsibility of calling their own plays. Still, I have never heard a coach say that the reason a quarterback was not allowed to call his own plays was because he was too damned dumb. Maybe the coaches think so, but I've never heard one say so.

In your case, if you've joined the growing ranks of goal seekers, you will be the only one calling your plays. There is no coach, no big brain on the sidelines to do your thinking for you.

A goal seeker *is* the quarterback on his own team. He (or she) must listen to advice from his players, observe the defense, then decide the play that best fits the game strategy.

If it is a bad call, the judgment was yours and only you are responsible. In this game of goal seeking, the result is determined totally by the quality of the plays that the quarterback calls. That's you.

It's *Your* Game

When you have decided it's time to play, your game is the only game in town for you! What a lot of would-be goal seekers fail to understand is that no matter how excited they get over working towards some particular goal, the rest of the world could give less than a damn. Even your own teammates, if this is a team operation, will not have the same degree of enthusiasm you have, since they are only paid to play. This is not to say they will not play hard or at least earn their pay, it's simply a fact of life. Even your wife, husband, boyfriend, or girlfriend won't be as enthused, though they are bound to benefit by your accomplishment (win). They may love you, but they just can't love your goals as much as you do.

This is so hard to understand it sometimes defeats the would-be goal seeker. In extreme cases, he may say aloud or to himself, "Why should I knock myself out? Nobody, not even my family, believes in me."

Well, that's just one more hurdle you have to get over fast. The serious player who sees an opportunity to gain something he wants and decides it's worth the risk, work and effort learns to button his lip and say no more than is necessary about his actions to those who are not directly involved and who thus have a limited interest. It may make you feel lonely not to be able to discuss your game with family and friends, but there are two reasons to clam up—to avoid premature discouragement and also for reasons of security. The fewer people who know your plans, the less chance that Murphy's Law can become operative.

I have spent a lot of time discussing team selection and team play, because I wanted you to know that it will be necessary to have help from others from time to time, but in seven out of ten cases, you will find it easier and more effective—at least in the first stages of a game—to play all by yourself.

For one thing, the game will go faster because you will not have to depend on other persons' schedules and can go as fast (or as slow) as you wish. You will also present a lower profile. Remember Sergeant York, the World War I sniper who single-handedly took out a whole nest of Germans? The enemy was looking for a platoon.

You will find that you can call on the service of free-agent specialists any time you need them, pay them for their work, and release them.

As for that running back, the legal eagle, call on his or her services to make the winning touchdown, but then only on the play that you call, and by the numbers—also within the time limit specified on the thirty-second clock. All too often, the lawyers want to make a simple play look too grandiose and you run out of time and lose a game.

I have witnessed failures in goal seeking that resulted for no other reason than that the players did not start at the beginning and follow one fundamental procedure. That procedure is to ask first for what you want more than once—as a matter of fact many times. More times than I can count, I have gotten something or somewhere because I kept letting it be known I was interested.

For example, I was interested in becoming part of a touring trade show and seminar program. I let several members of the production know that I was available, asking them what the booking procedure was and who I should contact. The answers were vague, and I got the impression that these folks weren't too interested in my joining. But as I was leaving, I happened to run into the promoter. I introduced myself and informed him of my interest. Within ten days, he called, and I became a featured portion of the tour. I simply ask!

Listen to Suggestions, but Make Up Your Own Mind

Everybody has an opinion on everything and anything and, when asked, they will give it to you. Your laws and in-laws will give you advice on how to raise children, whether you ask for it or not. They'll tell you how to treat their daughter or son. Your father will tell you how to succeed in business even if he's a bricklayer. Your mother will instruct you on what changes to make in your spouse's habits. You will never lack for advice.

Nobody, not even your own family, really wants you to become "bigger" than they are. It's not just selfishness or jealousy. They love you just the way you are and actually fear the changes that might come about in you through success. That is why, so often, the advice from both laws and in-laws is, "Yes, but that isn't for you."

The hell it isn't! Go after your goals, If you need advice from anyone, then seek out qualified scouts, weigh their information and then make your own decision. You will find the result easier to live with.

As a writer of many books and articles, I remain curious as I write as to whether I am communicating my ideas or information in a sincere, understandable way. Still, I have never let my wife or any other member of my family or any close friends read my manuscripts. Well there is one exception. Like Bennett Cerf, I never learned to type. I write in longhand and because grammar, spelling and punctuation are not my long suits, my transcriber—in this case my daughter—will ask me if I didn't mean to say it this way or that way. I will honor her question, but I'll say it my way. She will edit her typing for errors but not for content. That is left only to the experts, the editors.

When I first began to write, I was lucky. My very first book became a best seller, *Plants Are Like People*. Much of the credit goes to the publisher and his promotional people, but did I say I was lucky? Shame on me! One reason that book sold so big was because I got out into the field and worked my tail off to promote it. That was part of the game plan when I wrote the book.

Back to the point I was making: I heard a lot of sad stories from my editor about first-time writers who showed their manuscript to a best friend or relative and were told that it wouldn't sell. They became so discouraged they just put their pages away. Even sadder, the works of these writers have many times been picked up years later by competent evaluators, put into print and made into best sellers! Sometimes this has happened years after the author died.

Enough said about the value of advice. The value of any advice must be exactly equal to the quality and qualifications of the adviser.

Don't Be Afraid to Call Time Out

If at any time during a campaign or goal seeker's game you get the feeling that you are losing control of yourself or your team—if you or your players become tired or confused or a little depressed—take a timeout from the game.

Sometimes a game just gets moving too fast and you may not be ready with your next play (you may not have the money to close the deal yet, certain papers may not be ready, or a player you need may not yet be in place). Dozens of reasons may arise to make you decide to slow down a game. When you do so, take the opportunity to rechannel your efforts into some of the everyday chores you must do. When you're ready to move again, re-evaluate your position on the field, look over the opposing team and call time-in.

Calling time out can have still another, unexpected, advantage. I have on more than one occasion confused the defense by calling an unexpected time out at a critical time in the game. The goal of one of my games was hosting a local TV show. I was on the verge of signing for it when I found out that an opportunity to do a major national TV show was coming up in two days—the same day as the start of the local show. I called a friend who was on the road with another show and asked if he wanted a day off—I would fill in for him. He did. I did. And the national show came through for me. The delay also allowed me to sign to do the local show without an "exclusive" clause.

Remember the Game Plan

Remembering the game plan at all times is critical, and I want you to learn—and remember this well! There are critics of goal seeking who will say that concentration on the game plan contradicts the purpose and restricts the results. This kind of critic needs a plexiglass bellybutton, too.

First off, we are goal *seekers*, not mere goal *setters*. I've met many a goal setter and they just "set" there and wait for it to hatch. Goal *seekers* try to reach that which they keenly preview to be what they desire for themselves.

Naturally, many changes over which we have no control can occur during a game, so a good game plan has to be flexible enough to allow for adjustments. Quite often, changes have to be integrated into the game plan and then into the game itself, but that's no reason to knock game-planning. The sad part is that even the critics of game-planning agree with me on one thing—that we all need goals to guide us if we are to accomplish anything more than a mundane existence.

Setting a goal is like setting a table. It doesn't do a damned bit of good unless you've also planned a meal.

Next, let me remind you that it is not a mortal sin, nor should it cause an ego-crushing psychological wound if you should lose a few games. If after you lose one you feel guilty or go moping around, you'll just be carrying defeat into your next game.

Your security is in yourself and in your ability to make things happen for you, because you know what abilities you have and which ones you lack. One talent you should never lack is the ability to recruit people who have the abilities you don't have and who will apply them on your behalf, for a price.

Some critics of scientific game-planning will say it takes too much time. Nonsense! The goal seeker is working within the time that has been allotted and knows that the time factor is "x" (God is the only one who knows its quantity). That means we should make a reasonable attempt to schedule our goals. Every goal needs a time frame—when work toward it should begin and when it should be achieved. Don't let your seeking drag on forever!

Always use the **KISS** (**K**eep **I**t **S**imple **S**tupid) method. Set an honest and reasonable time in which to play the game to reach your goal. So much for time. As for space, there are no out-of-bounds areas in the goal-seeker's game. It can be played locally, nationally, or globally. It just depends on what league you play in.

Don't Get Your Signals Crossed

I have touched on this a little bit in a couple of different places in this book, but now I want to stress how important the understanding of assignments and timing can be. If you are playing a game alone and only using free agents for specialty work, then it is only necessary for you to refer to your game plan and the proximity of the ball (you) to your goal and make sure you don't get too jumpy as you near the goal line. It's an awful temptation when you get close to those goldplated goal posts to queer a play because you have gotten too anxious. At such times the defense can read you wrong. Just take the time you have allotted yourself to achieve the goal. Play as if everything is on schedule. Follow your game plan, and you'll be less liable to make a mistake.

Here is an example: I knew that if I could present one of my propositions to the chief operating officer (COO) of a corporation, I could end up making the deal I wanted. The defense put up to block me was so tight (because a few key defensive players were sure it was going to cost them their jobs) that it seemed almost impossible to stay within the rules I had set for myself. I went back to my head scout and said, "O.K., find me a weakness." What he found was not actually a weakness but a kindness. The COO and his wife had a great interest in a certain charity and she was an ardent gardener and president of her local garden club. I was also informed that the charity was having a fund-raising dinner soon in a much-touted restaurant. The new owner of that place was an acquaintance, so needless to say, I bought a ticket to that gala affair where I was introduced to the COO and his wife. She owned a couple of my books and indeed, was a fan of mine. Her husband offered to buy me a drink, and in our conversation I mentioned how I had tried in vain to contact him on a business proposal.

"Now is as good a time as any," he said, so we went off into a corner and talked it over. The next day, I won my game. To answer your question, no, none of the defense lost a thing. To the contrary, those guys who were going to block me actually gained by the move and are today among my strongest advocates. It's just that I never gave them a chance to play while I was seeking my goal.

Concentrate on the Goal

Oftentimes in what starts out as well-planned goal seeking, some worthwhile objectives get lost in the fervor of the game. Hey, friend! It's the truth. I know, I've been there more times than I like to remember—both as a quarterback on my own team and as a player on other teams. The game just gets so all-fired exciting and the enthusiasm becomes so intense that when the game is over we've forgotten what in the hell it was we were playing for. It sounds impossible and silly, but it's true.

Put your present goals on paper and list them in the order of their importance. Then post them in conspicuous places like on your shaving or vanity mirror, on the visor of your car or in your wallet.

A mirror, incidentally, is an ideal place to post your goals. That way you'll see yourself and the goal at the same time!

Don't Pass to a Fumbler Twice

Does this seem like a cruel rule? It isn't. There is a lot of difference between a blocked pass, an incompletion, a finger-tip juggle, and a good old-fashioned fumble. There isn't one coach I've ever met who has ever said there is any reason for a ball carrier to fumble if he carries the ball in the prescribed fundamental way, but ball players all get style-conscious—and that's when they get sloppy and fumble.

If I pay a person to play and that individual gets sloppy and fumbles the ball, even if one of the other team members is fortunate enough to recover the ball, I'll never let that player carry the ball again, at least not in this game. Another time, maybe, another game, but not in this one.

I'm talking here about the player who fumbles only once. There is also the chronic fumbler whom I never want to see again in any game. Efficiency experts in the big manufacturing corporations know how to identify the chronic fumbler. If a worker makes a first error, he or she gets another chance, but if the same error occurs over and over again, it's called "the repeatable error." If you commit enough of those in a big factory, not even the union steward can save you.

When I am on the run, I cover up that ball with my hands, feet, head, and body. When I go down, it hurts, but I've still got the ball.

Mix 'n Match Your Plays

If you watch the professional football teams on TV each Sunday, you will soon observe why some teams, guided by a versatile coach and a confident quarterback, constantly win while others are destined for the second division. In most cases, the not-so-flexible teams run the first and second down and pass on the third. Very soon the defense sets up.

When the quarterback has confidence in his own ability and knows all his players, when he has the game plan well in mind and has earned the confidence of the coach and the staff, he will run a defense ragged. You see, he won't be following a "pattern" to any great extent, but he *will* be following his basic game plan. The game plan influences his calls as he mixes and matches his plays and keeps the defense where it belongs—on the defensive.

That is precisely what you must learn to do. Don't feel that there is any *order* in which you must approach a goal. If you have confidence in your own ability and reason, then do the unexpected when it's unexpected and keep the pressure on. You will soon run the defense crazy.

I once worked with a police crew chief on nights when I was a young officer. This old chief had more solid busts (arrests) and convictions to his credit than anybody else, and the reason was that he never did what was expected. It was always the unexpected—like two of us hiding in a shipping crate that was delivered—with us in it—right to the bad guys' headquarters. We sat in there until we were able to overhear the hoods' plans for the night. We then gave a prearranged signal: Using a box lid as a flag, we signaled a lookout outside the building. A marked scout car arrived and we made the bust. The new information we had gathered gave us a solid case.

Lesson: Know when to do the unexpected and the unexpected won't happen to you.

Test the Opposition's Defenses

Your scouts may be good, but there's no way to prepare against a sudden change in management, financial switches, or attitude changes on the part of certain defensive players. So, be cautious, test the defense with a good variety of tactics. Test until you can read it. Then plunge ahead and stick to your game plan. Stay within your rules. Always try to complete the game in a shorter period of time than you have set. Speed can be an asset, but *haste* never. The faster you go, the harder you'll be to follow, but never go so fast (hastily) that you forget caution and lose control of the ball. Keep the game moving at a pace that is comfortable, and remember that your team can't go any faster than you can.

Run If You Have To

There's a difference between running smart and running scared. There are also times when it's smart to run away . . . like when everybody is covered and the defense is ready to pound your butt three feet into the ground. Friend, you've got no choice but to run! If possible, run for daylight. If not, pick out a key defensive player and the best possible cover-up, but don't try to eliminate him. Try for prolonged or step-by-step elimination.

I have had men and women come up to me and express down-right fear of some other person in the business community, stating that they wouldn't dare address that person, let alone work against his or her wishes.

Now get this! There is NO legitimate man or woman in the business world for you to be afraid of or to hesitate to do business with or go into competition against. You may be awed by a person's position or power or accumulated wealth, but if you have something they want, they'll get it the same way they got what they already have. The same rule holds true for you.

I have had the intimidation style used against me by some unscrupulous power merchants, but it didn't take me long to even the score. The technique often used is called, "Let it all hang out." Do it yourself or tell your scouts to open all the closet doors and shake down Mr. Big from the top of his head to his toenails and, lo and behold, they will usually come back with ashes and bones from years ago. In response to one of the biggest intimidation jobs I ever had tried on me—threats from the CEO of a company I wanted to acquire—I simply sent a copy of a scouting report (an arrest record that was less than flattering to the CEO) to the right place along with a copy of my game plan. That won the game. I call it meeting intimidation with "*out*-timidation!"

Don't Pass with a Sore Arm

I was going to say don't consider the sore-arm parallel as a strictly physical thing. Then I decided that what I'm going to talk about is really quite physical. I'm talking about that certain "gut feeling" that every professional claims to have at some time or other when making a final decision on some crucial point.

There are no reliable statistics on how often gut feeling has been the deciding force in the won-loss records. Now and then you'll hear a winner talk about "gut feeling" but more often nobody wants to admit that the result came from anything less than a planned program, superior training or a "calculated risk."

Have I ever relied on my own gut feelings? I'll never tell, but I will give you a little word of advice that might be a give-away. If, after you listen to your scouts, talk to your players, design your game plan, and start to call a play . . . if, at that moment, something doesn't *feel* right, don't pass. Run the damned thing out of bounds or cover up the ball and drop. It really is a lot like having a sore arm. That arm may have plenty of strength in it, but whatever is making it hurt will probably affect your aim. You don't know why. You just know that it does.

Gut feelings, when they come, are almost always of a negative nature. They are warnings, vague feelings that say, "You ain't ready, Bud!" Such feelings won't come very often if you have covered all of the proper points of preparation.

As for going ahead and trying to make yardage on the basis of a "gut feeling," what would you really rather rely on, your gut or your brain? Your gut or that plan you worked out so nicely? I think you know the answer.

Chapter 10

Play to Win, Not to Please the Crowd

It's fourth down, one yard to go for the first down. The crowd is calling, "Go, go, go!" The quarterback calls for the punt and now the fans begin to boo! That's a scene that is played over and over throughout the football season.

The lesson to be learned here is that you don't listen to the crowd when it comes time to play and make the big, important decisions. The spectators at any game don't have anything to lose but their tempers. While it's always nice to hear applause, it's a whole lot nicer to win the game.

Too many persons let their actions be influenced by the wishes of others, only to find themselves on the short end of the stick in the end. Since it's your goal, you make the decision without any thought as to what others might do if they were in your shoes.

The reason is simple. They are NOT in your shoes. Let's hope they never are!

Don't Ever Believe a Soothsayer

A great number of my acquaintances practically make a religion of reading their daily horoscopes in the paper, or have a monthly chart made for them, while others punch up their so-called bio-rhythm for the day on their handy dandy bio-rhythm computers. All that jazz is supposed to tell them where their heads, hearts, and bodies are supposed to be for the day.

Some of them get the shakes over certain numbers that show up. The really serious cases get their palms read or let someone fish through a dirty teacup for omens. For centuries people have used potions, motions, and lotions trying to look into the future. If you know what's good for you and your future, you will avoid all of this tomfoolery when it comes to pursuing your goals. Don't look to the stars for guidance or you may just wind up losing your own Star Wars. Fortune tellers make fortunes for themselves, and nobody else.

I am so against this sort of thing that I will leave a room if someone insists on reading my fortune. Those who profess this stuff, of course, will insist it's scientific and accuse me of being afraid to listen for fear what they predict might come true.

That's nonsense! I've got brains enough to know that anything the ear hears, the eye casts upon, the nose smells, or the hands feel goes into your super computer, the mind. When it comes time to make a decision on any specific matter, anything that is even remotely stored in your brain is punched up for you to consider in making your decision—even that junk you just heard. Just by chance, you might let it influence your decision and that would be one hell of an error on the part of a hard-playing goal seeker.

Because the brain *is* a computer, it will pay you to program it like any other computer. You know the old computer operator's warning that's spelled GIGO. GIGO means "Garbage In, Garbage Out."

Oh sure, I know that some of the biggest stars in Hollywood and even some stock-market analysts play around with astrology, but a lot of that is publicity flak. It's written for the boobs. A more typical story is that of a recognizable personality, an acquaintance of mine, who has maybe "done all right" but has never made it to the top of the pile where he has the potential to be. One reason is because he's involved in star-gazing. If the "stars aren't right," according to his soothsayer, he will not move on a goal. When intelligent people do things like this, I really believe they're just looking for excuses—any excuse—for not exercising their talents.

As a consumer marketing consultant serving many national companies, I was once asked by a major manufacturer to suggest a television spokesperson for his line of products. It didn't take me five seconds to answer. I knew just the personality. He was right for the product and would give the whole line a strong recognition factor. I'd really like to print his name for you because you'd know it instantly from watching TV, although you never saw him working for my client.

Don't let me drag this story out. When I mentioned the name of the performer, my client was as pleased as a new papa. He could see the continuity immediately. Could we get this guy? What was his price? Did I know him?

Yes, I knew him personally and I knew he could use the exposure and the money, so I called him and asked him how he felt about doing a national commercial. I didn't, however, tell him the name of the company or the product line. His reply was, "Boy, wouldn't I!"

"O.K.," I said, "You call this gentleman." I gave him the number and a specific time to call. I knew he could put together a nice package and he assured me that he would do it, so I called my client and gave him the good news.

A week later, I received a phone call from my client who was not just a little upset. He was a lot upset because this prize personality of mine had not called and, furthermore, would not return his calls.

I then rushed through a call to my performer and asked, "What the hell is going on? You assured me you would call my client!"

"Well," he answered, "I called my astrologer and she said that because my lip was on the cusp (cuspidor or whatever) I should wait for a more propitious day to call."

"You've got to be kidding," I said.

"Oh, no, Jerry! I'm serious."

The end of the story is that I got my knuckles rapped and my would-be TV personality is still a quarter of a million dollars short of what he could have had. He realized his mistake, but I hate to tell you what he did about it.

He changed astrologers.

No Premature Publicity

As you progress in goal seeking, you are bound to make a little noise in the career or business community in which you play. The more wins you chalk up, the louder the impact and the more interest you will create for the media, TV, radio, and newspapers. Getting on an important talk show, for example, is especially flattering and ego-feeding, but beware of giving away your plans prematurely or you will sure as hell find the opposition ready and waiting to knock you off your publicity pedestal. Indeed, if you expose some particularly attractive plan to a million or more people through the media, you might just get yourself a million more opponents than you need!

Any Publicity Is Good Publicity

What a crock that is! I'm sure that if P. T. Barnum were here, he would like to eat those famous words of his. "I don't care what they say about me," he said, "just as long as they mention my name." I am sure that after that big fire in the Big Top a few years back in which many adults and children died, Mr. Barnum would have liked to have had them forget his name.

If it is in your power to play within your rules, you will have no reason to regret your publicity. Just remember this word of advice whenever you're talking with media people:

Nothing is off the record!

Granted that everything you say may not make the immediate news, but it *will* show up in the future as hearsay from another source.

There Is No Such Thing as a Tie

A tie to me has always seemed like a waste of time. A lot of effort expended for a result that doesn't count. In business, if the opposition offers to merge or give you a smaller portion of the profits than you had set as your goal, and you accept, even though you know that you have the stamina and resources to go all the way and win, then it's a tie, and you will never amount to a tinker's dam.

A tie is worse than a loss because in a tie you will never know who could have won. In business, a tie is simply a stalemate where neither side has controlling interest. If you can't get control, take a profit and move on. If you think you are losing and accept a tied situation as some kind of stop-loss move, it's no good. If you let it happen, the other side will always control that goal and eventually you will lose it. Play to win. If you lose, you gave it your best shot; there are no strings attached, and you can come back for a replay when you are ready. A tie, in another definition, is a rope. Don't get yourself tied up!

Never Announce Your Lineup in Advance

Even though we are using football as an analogy, we must still tailor the idea to fit the principle. I am not going to display my power until the time comes for the two teams to come out onto the playing field. Never show your hand in advance if it is at all possible to avoid it. Always keep in mind that we are not playing the game of goal seeking for the spectators; in business this translates to the media and any non-involved persons. The smaller the crowd of observers, the safer your style and strategy will be. I've seldom seen a crowd at a big game that didn't contain a scout or two from some team coming up on the schedule later in the season.

Does Everybody Have a Price?

Now here's a proposition that has been and will be discussed forever! Those who say, "Yes, everybody has his price," will give you the example of the Disciple who sold out Christ. Those who say "no" put in a qualification: they say it has to do with the weakness and greed of the individual. I agree with the latter. Theoretically, there should be persons in this world who will never sell out, but how will you ever know? No matter how high the price, there's always a higher price. We can point with joy to some members of the human race who wouldn't sacrifice their principles for a billion bucks, but for ten billion . . . ? You'll never know!

I have had it happen to me. People of whom I would never have dreamed it possible have sold out on me. In most cases their reason was to gain a short-term profit and take care of some unforeseen situation. Yet I felt deceived, totally. I saw red, but no . . . I did not act or speak until I had assessed the damage and changed the game plan. What else did I do? I did exactly what I have advised you to do. I never hit the bastards but I have put their names on my big bad black list.

So, how do you avoid the possibility of someone selling out on you? Keep you eyes and ears open . . . and, pray a lot.

Minority Balance? Bah, Humbug!

When I put a team together, I never give any thought to race, religion, nationality or sex. I go for the players who can accomplish the assignments I have to make, with the least amount of effort and in the most efficient way possible to get the most profitable results. I've seen times when five players on a six-person team were women. All professional goal seekers have certain men and women whose wisdom they respect, either as players or as counsel.

Speaking of counsel, you can often recruit a lot higher on the social scale in that department than you can for actual players. I'm talking about folks who have been all the way up there, who can give you reliable psychological interpretations of thoughts. Such persons as a rule will not be asked to be players because they are considered far above the playing field for most games. That doesn't mean they are saints (and as a rule they won't be clergymen). Your best counsellors will be highly successful professional or business persons and when you get up into that strata, you'll find that success is color-blind, sexless, and without religious preference.

I have a couple of super-stars when it comes to getting good goal seeking counsel. One is black, Dr. J. Tyson Tildon of the University of Maryland, head of pediatric research and author of a book that every goal seeker should read, *The Anglo-Saxon Agony.** The other is a white man, Bob Morris, an ultra-successful businessman and entrepreneur. My two great counsellors have never met.

Gray matter is always the same color no matter what kind of skin it comes wrapped in. And, brains don't have sex organs. Go for the best and don't let anything except results influence your choice of players or counsel.

---

*Tildon, J. Tyson. *The Anglo-Saxon Agony*. Philadelphia, PA: Whitmore Publishing Co., 1972.

Don't Play out of Your Class

Your class? If you think I am implying that there are those who are better than you are, settle down! No one human being is better than another. We were all created equal and we will all go out equal, no matter what we accomplish or acquire, no matter how large or small the crowd that comes to our funerals or how ornate our gravesite.

However, when it comes to going one-on-one or team-for-team in a goal seeking game, you bet your bippy there are those who are better than you are—more experienced, better financed and better able to muster more physical resources than you can.

I could write on this subject until my fingers are bloody and there are those of you who will argue, but I learned the hard way and so will you.

Don't Give away Anything for Nothing

Oh, sure, if you want to give away a box of candy or a bunch of flowers, I approve that kind of generosity, but I'm advising you to be stingy when it comes to giving away advice and services. You will be plagued by people who want to know how to get ahead with a project or get out of a sticky business situation. You will be presented with a multitude of "can you solve my problem?" situations.

Unless it's a member of the family, I suggest that you remember all of your fundamental goal seeker's training and make sure that everyone pays cash or something of equivalent value. No, it's not being mercenary. If you ask any of these same people to perform their services for nothing, they would think you were nuts. Then why shouldn't the same hold true for your services as a goal seeker with a reputation for success?

I know an advertising man who prepared a sales brochure for two thousand dollars. While he was with his client, the client asked, "What kind of sales contest would put this company ahead?" The advertising man, still all warm inside from that $2,000 brochure sale, said, "Forget the sales contest. You're selling heavy machinery on bids, so why not run a contest for the largest number of specifications for bids turned in by a salesman?" Now, two thousand bucks for writing a brochure isn't bad, but that advertising character actually gave away a million dollar idea for nothing! The contest for bids really worked and, as you know, once a company has specifications on everything the market is going to buy, the rest is easy. On the basis of that one idea, the manufacturer doubled his annual volume. It's enough to make a grown man cry. And, please take note that I, Jerry Baker, am not telling you everything I've learned for nothing either. You paid for it in the price of this book. I am retained by many large companies who pay me well for my opinions and advice. I am also paid to lecture on what I have learned through experience. So, charge ahead—but charge for everything!

Who Asked You?

Everything in a goal seeker's professional life works both ways. Your career path is a two-way street and you must therefore practice what you preach. Now after telling you not to give away advice when it's asked for, I am going to tell you to resist the temptation to give advice when it's *not* asked for. Just as you shouldn't listen to folks who start out saying, "If I were you . . . ," you should resist the urge to say, "If you ask me . . ."—when nobody did.

Don't offer advice to anyone with whom you are associated in the business world unless and until you are asked—and then put a price on it. It will save both you and the other party a great deal of embarrassment.

Even when you *are* solicited for an opinion, consider the subject matter, the person asking, and the sensitivity of the subject as it pertains to any of your present goals. You have to ask yourself if the opinion or advice you give can be held against you. I mean if you advise a guy to jump off a bridge and he drowns, you have incurred some kind of liability by advising him. I'm not trying to be funny and I don't want to seem overly suspicious, but I am darned cautious if any information I give could come back to haunt me in the form of a defense against me. Also, before giving an opinion or advice, I do what I told you to do in the last section. I figure out what it's worth and put a price on it. If I decide it's not worth anything, I keep it to myself.

A good answer to give when advice is requested and you don't want to give it, question the value of what you have to offer, or suspect that the asker won't pay for it is, "Sir, I think you should ask someone with more knowledge of the subject than I have."

Sometimes you're going to be just busting to tell people what you know, but if nobody asks you, keep your lip buttoned. If the subject is any of your business, you'll do better to spend your time listening.

Don't Worry about the Spectators, They Always Get Their Money's Worth

If your game is a big one and involves you with well known players, you are bound to attract attention. There will be both partisan and non-partisan folks out there looking on, but you're going to have to ignore all of them while you concentrate on the game. Remember that the *spectators have nothing invested in their seats*, but you stand a chance to lose yours! So when the press asks for comments, your most positive response will be a negative.

Never Take A Guilt Trip

In the early stages of goal seeking you will experience some feelings of guilt, not because you deserve it but because you invite it. That's right, you bring it on yourself, or it is pushed upon you.

It is really important that you recognize early in this career of goal seeking to identify false guilt and real guilt and avoid them both. Either one, if not checked quickly, can cause you to lose.

False guilt is presented to you by someone else who wishes to control you by implying that what you are about to do or are doing is selfish and for your own pleasure or well-being. Example: A spouse who tells you to go ahead with a decision to do something new or different—"don't worry about me." You should never feel guilty nor rescind a decision for this type of guilt.

On the other hand, the threat of *real guilt* should be a neon "stop" sign. If your plans or your actions would prevent another person from earning a living, inhibit his or her creative expression, interfere with that individual's happiness, family well-being, or in any way endanger his or her life or health—stop. I'm not too concerned about your becoming involved with *real guilt*, because if you are playing by the eleven guides we call rules, you won't entertain a game plan that would include underhanded strategies.

I am, however, very concerned about your reactions and actions as they apply to *false guilt*. Crying, swearing, threats of reprisal, screaming, silence, withholding of affections, accusations are all tools or signs of false guilt application. If it's not deserving then don't accept it or let it interfere. Because if you do, it then becomes real guilt for the person inflicting it.

Part IV
Fourth Quarter

Chapter 11

Keep a Close Eye on Players' Performances and Psycho-physical Conditions

"**H**e is a big boy and he can look out for himself." This is what is usually said when one adult offers advice for another through a mutual friend.

As a goal-seeker quarterback, it is your responsibility to keep your eyes open at all times during the game for any signs of mental or physical fatigue in your players. They may be big boys, but it pays to look after them. It may be their health, but it's your time, so make their condition your business. Besides, it's often the really big boy or girl who is *least* likely to look out for himself or herself.

As a goal seeker, even though you recognize the need to be selfish in order to be a winner, you must be generous with concern for the condition of other players. Otherwise your team could fall apart before your eyes. On the pages that follow, I'll be giving you some of the signs to be alert to in making sure your team stays all in one piece.

The Older Players Can Get Carried Away in More than One Way

This manure that they spread around that "you are only as old as you feel" can do nothing but get a lot of innocent people hurt. Up north where I live, I hate to see the first snowfall of the season come, because many of our older and experienced members of society grab the snow shovel and head for the snowbanks that are blocking the drive. Then, instead of finding themselves behind the wheel of the family car, they end up flat on their backs in the intensive care unit of the local hospital. That is, if they live. They simply put too much pressure on their fifty-, sixty-, or seventy-amp bodies and blew a fuse. Those of you who, like myself, use a great number of the older and more experienced players, should take into consideration the age of the equipment they're working with and design your game plan in such a way you don't endanger them. By the way, don't leave it up to them to tell you when they need a rest or it's time for the locker room. Many of them wouldn't tell you if their lives depended on it—which well might be the case.

As a humorous aside, one older man I worked with says most guys over forty don't have to worry about heart attacks shoveling snow—"Your back will go first!"

Make it Exercise Not Punishment

Over the years I have watched friends and acquaintances wake up to the fact that they have not properly exercised their muscles and find that they have an obvious case of "Dunn Loops" disease, that's when your tummy done looped over your belt. This is caused by a diet too heavy in seafood: you eat all the food you see! Or, as a friend of mine said, he's involved with Weight Watchers, "His weight is all out front where he can watch it." This is intended to be humorous, even if it is corny. What is not funny is going to a funeral of a long-time friend, who finally admitted that he had a problem with his weight and without proper supervision commenced a diet and exercise program that was too strenuous. As for yourself, make good health a goal and include nutrition and exercise in your game plan. But make darn sure your first team member is your doctor.

Be Alert for the Stress Points

I am sure that this may sound like an ominous warning, and those of you under forty may feel that it is only of concern to the older goal seekers.

Like hell! Stress has no pet sex or age group. The only exception would be that older players are more likely to suffer the most severe consequences. That's because they have less physical capacity to resist the gut punch called stress. Don't kid yourself into the false security of thinking that stress can't injure or slow up a younger person. Olympic Skating Champion Dorothy Hamill was just twenty-one years old and a big showbiz success. Dorothy drank a lot of milk, but not just for the vitamins. She had an ulcer . . . from stress.

As a goal seeker, you will always be exposed to heavy stress. If you begin to feel physically tight, grinding your teeth, bearing down extra hard with your pen or pencil, talking faster than normal, or getting numb in the ass, watch out! Get off by yourself and get in a comfortable position sitting on the floor with your back leaning against the wall. Shut your eyes. Now, starting from your toes and working up to your face and jaws, try hard to relax. I mean *really* relax. Breathe normally through your nose. Don't take big deep breaths through your mouth or you will drive all the carbon dioxide out of your lungs (we need to retain some CO_2) and you will begin to hyperventilate (gasp). Count aloud from one to twenty-five, one number at a time, each time you exhale. Then, start over. Keep it up for fifteen minutes (yes, you *can* spare the time!). When outside thoughts interfere, start your count again. You will now begin to feel super-relaxed. Soon you feel that you are ready to go back into action. I have been in games that were so intense, I have had to practice what I'm preaching here as often as four times a day.

Yes, if a goal is worth working for, sometimes it's worth *resting* for. A rest today can get you *all* the rest tomorrow!

Young and Inexperienced Players Tend to Try to Take the Bit in Their Teeth

This is by no means a criticism of youth, but it is a word of advice both for you owner-quarterbacks calling your own goal-seeking game and for younger players just learning the sport.

This advice is especially hard to take if you're young and independent of nature, but when you are assigned a person to make contact with or to take out of the play, control yourself. Don't get too aggressive and don't try to reinvent the wheel. Have confidence in the coaching staff. Trust the information you got from the scouts. Respect the decisions that were the basis for the game plan and do what you're told . . . whether it's something somebody else told you to do or something you told *yourself* to do. Do it. Stick with the plan! Don't make a snap decision that someone else or something else is more important, because if the quarterback gets blind-sided by your man, you may just have to run faster from your own teammate than from the opposition.

The Perfect Blend

If there is any such thing as a perfect blend in a people machine, it's having younger players assigned to do the fancy-footed plays and older more experienced players to look after the strategic matters. You need the young guys for those quick raids out into the secondary defense positions (middle management defensive positions) because it's the cats in those positions who are most likely to act without thinking and end up clipping you. A younger player can usually recover faster from hard contact. Though I have a couple of seventy-year-old dudes who can make O.J. Simpson's footwork look clumsy by comparison, they save it for the tight spots. I play these old guys sparingly, but when it comes to doing the head work near the goal line, you have to use the most experienced players you have, the kind who can cut back and innovate in a clutch. This only comes from experience. In short, nobody's ever too young or too old to play—if they know their stuff.

It isn't just blends of young and old that work well. Often, it's a blend of sexes. I have found, for example, that if I team up an older woman with a younger man I get spectacular results with very few injuries. No, I have never had any problems I couldn't handle with a reverse team-up. That is, older man/younger woman. Maybe a broken heart once in awhile, but that's considered a minor injury for a goal seeker.

Everything Is Your Business

When you are playing for your own marbles, everything that could cause you to lose them is your business. A lot of things about other people that may seem to be none of your business can be very much your business . . . such matters as their health, romances, and finances. You also want to know what they're saying about you and about the game. Now, if you think this is being a little nosey, you're right. Indeed, it helps to be more than a little nosey.

For example, if I hear a player isn't feeling well and brace that player on the question, I get more than a little PO'd if he beats around the bush. Any player who is having problems in the romance department may be unable to concentrate on his or her assignment. As for the talkers, I've got a big club ready for the big mouth, the character who discusses my business in public places and it gets back to me. Bars, planes and trains are no places to discuss anything the enemy could be interested in.

Other people's finances are my business, too, as they should be your business. That's because any player who gets in over his wallet can be a prime target for a bribe. Furthermore, anybody who gets a personal reputation as a deadbeat or paper-hanger attracts too much attention.

All these cautions apply to your own personal conduct as well.

You May Not Always be Right in Your Calls, But It's Your Game

Here's a little play on an old saying: The boss may not always be right but he is always the boss. It's true. You can't always be right, but since you stand to lose or gain the most, it's only right that the other players bow to your judgment.

I am not suggesting a hard-headed and stubborn approach. I am merely saying that the last word is yours. Yes, I have the greatest respect for anyone I select to play for me and I will listen to his or her suggestions at any time. I might even follow those suggestions right out the window. But please remember that whatever decision I make, it is my decision—and I call the play.

Chapter 12

Ups and Downs are
Par for the Course

If Women Have a Handicap
in Business, It's Men

In June of 1927 there was a national conference held in Cincinnati, Ohio, by some of the nation's leading physicians in the field of mental hygiene. The theme of the conference was "Why Men Fail" in business and Dr. Anita M. Miihl, a psychiatrist, delivered a paper on "Why Women Fail." What I found most interesting in her report (over sixty years old) was that women at that time had fewer problems to overcome in achieving success than men did. Dr. Miihl stated that women's handicaps in business are not physical, but totally psychological. Here are her reasons women have difficulty succeeding in business: Business is controlled by men; Women approach business with the wrong state of mind; Women are more emotional than men; Women are thought of as "the opposite sex"; Women do not dress for success; Women are unduly "touchy"; Women have an unquenchable desire to mother the weak; Most married women hold back in business to avoid overshadowing their husbands; Women regard work as a mere substitute activity until marriage; Women are not as aggressive as men.

I was so intrigued by this list that in 1985 I sent it to more than a hundred male business executives and asked them to indicate whether they agree or disagree with each statement. Nearly all the men responded. Here, in percentages, is how they agreed or disagreed:

Ten Reasons Women Fail in Business	Agree	Disagree
1. Business is controlled by men.	87%	13%
2. Women approach business with the wrong state of mind.	74%	26%
3. Women are more emotional than men.	72%	28%
4. Women are thought of as "the opposite sex."	28%	72%
5. Women do not dress for success.	23%	77%
6. Women are unduly "touchy."	83%	17%
7. Women have an unquenchable desire to mother the weak.	63%	37%
8. Most married women hold back in business to avoid overshadowing their husbands.	86%	14%
9. Women regard work as a mere substitute activity until marriage.	57%	43%
10. Women are not as aggressive as men.	61%	39%

As the song goes, "You've come a long way baby" but from the looks of my survey you still have a long way to go, if you are willing to accept these attitudes at face value.

A goal seeker is a goal seeker and sex has no bearing. You can still use this information to your advantage when picking a team and designing a game plan, but you must remember, as hard as it may be, never, never let vengeance be the motivator.

Most Men Are Terrified of Successful Women

This statement is really an extension of the husband being threatened by a wife who is more successful than he. I have to chuckle at the "cola bottle" executives who consider women inferior and are constantly commenting that women would not make good corporate timber because they are too emotional, physically weaker, lack the mental capacity of men, are gossipy, vindictive, and lack imagination beyond current fashions. Unfortunately for you women, between ninety-three percent and ninety-seven percent of the corporate executives in a 1981 survey hold most if not all of the above opinions.

It is a real asset to the goal seeker to have executives who hold such opinions on the opposing side. If you are a female goal seeker, it is a double advantage. How? They underrate your abilities and put up a weaker defense. Most of my male colleagues consider women to be among the brightest and toughest competitors. I find it an advantage to have more women on my team when the opposing team is a male group.

You Can't Let Her Do That, She's a Woman!

If I've had this warning thrown at me once, I've had it a hundred times. But one of my rules is that all players play equally. If your position calls for you to perform certain duties and that play is called, you go, Daddy-O—man, or woman. You see, I would never send a player out if I was not sure that man or woman couldn't complete the play.

I don't know whether this is the place to mention this or whether you're stupid enough to need the advice, but one of my rules is that I will never supply sex to accomplish my goals. If I find out that sex is the price, I can use it as ammunition against my foe and win hands-down, hands-off, or however you want to describe it.

My daughters like to call me a male chauvinist pig, but they always smile when they say it. Now, you know one reason why. I do enjoy being a gentleman.

One-on-One, Man against Woman in Business, She Will Win

I am constantly being called a champion of women's rights and, boy, are they right! Women deserve every opportunity, consideration, membership, wage, title and position available to men and any man who is opposed to this premise is totally insecure. He, no doubt, is afraid to compete with a woman one-on-one since he is doubtful of his own abilities.

When a woman competes with a man, all things being equal (education, experience and age), in seven out of ten cases the woman will win. The arguments about women being more emotional than men is hogwash! I have seen more emotional outbursts by men in business than women. I mean the screaming, stomping, crying and swearing.

So, as a goal seeker picking a team, look to and pay for the services of women. If you're a woman goal seeker, don't worry about balancing your team with men merely for the sake of appearance. Only qualifications and performance count; not sex.

Drugs are Dumb

It's short and sweet. If you need help to get up for the game, or down after, don't play for me. In the crowd I travel with, you sometimes need a score card to tell you who is playing with a full deck and when. I almost crowned one of my best players because he was eating M&M's.

Speaking of pills, I know a lot of supposedly upper-class people and celebrities think it's smart to fool around with cocaine and other "fashionable" drugs, but I was on the narcotics squad long enough to know that any kind of drug is trouble. The smart goal seeker doesn't take this stuff, nor does he score it for anybody else, regardless of the temptation. It's even worse than the sex ploy. Fool around with drugs and you will become, not a goal seeker but a "gaol" seeker. Gaol, in case the pun doesn't punch you right away, is the Welsh word for "jail."

It's Not a Sin to be Scared

Every person has his or her own definition of fright. Mine is that feeling I get just before a curtain goes up, or just before I open a newspaper knowing that a critic has reviewed one of my books—

or the feeling I get just before I let the opposition know I am coming out to play for the marbles.

Some doctors say it is the adrenalin in your system adjusting for the up-coming stress or strain. I call it the fight-or-run syndrome. It is *not* a sign of weakness. That is, if you fight!

Let Every Player Celebrate in His or Her Own Way and Time

I have never been one to enjoy a big loud victory celebration. I prefer to go off and have a quiet dinner with my wife and perhaps another couple. While some like a big hoopla, others greet the victory in funny, personal ways. They may even cry, or laugh, or giggle, or just go off by themselves. You never can predict what a good player will do once the pressure is off. So, show your appreciation but don't force a celebration on your team.

Stop Preparing for Failure

I have said that success or failure begins with your mother's attitudes and attention towards you from birth to five or six years of age. At that time of your life you can learn anything and you are eager to learn. It has been proven that infants can be taught several different languages all at one time when they are as young as six months, and not only languages, but all sorts of subjects. Why not teach them then to succeed, not fail? You did not read wrong; I'm saying that most mothers begin to prepare children for failure early in life when they say things like, "Look out, you're going to fall!" If you are close by to help them avoid pain, but not the fall and, when they do fall, make a statement like, "Let's try it again"—then a child will learn to take the falls in life as a lesson in how to succeed. If your mother didn't teach you that, it will be hard at first for you to regain your lost confidence. When a play falls apart, simply wipe away the tears, take a deep breath, look to see what went wrong, and correct it. Then plunge back into the fray. You'll soon stop preparing for failure, because there won't be any.

There Is No Blame For a Loss,
but You Have to Live with It

If you have to fault anyone, fault yourself. If you lose a goal you'll be tempted to blame somebody besides yourself. Don't. Don't blame yourself either. Maybe you really did screw it up, but indulging in self-recrimination won't do you any good, so forget it.

If you lost a goal-seeker's game, odds are you lost because the other team was better at that game. Review every aspect of that game and find the weak spots. Maybe it was another player who lost it for you, but the fault is still yours if you didn't bounce him off the squad. Aw, hell! Go ahead and lick your wounds if it makes you feel any better. Now get into training for that next game!

Don't Let Any Day Be a Blue One

I know it sounds easy to say, but avoiding the blues is another thing. Still, it isn't hard if you remember that feeling sad and sorry for yourself is wasted time. If you're down in the dumps for no reason you can think of—I mean if you are not physically or mentally ill— that is a total waste of time!

How do you lift your spirits? Well, first, you don't lift any of *those* kind of spirits! If you feel so bad you need a drink, you really need a doctor. No, what I do is first go to some place that has a great deal of activity going on, like a popular restaurant or club. Then I take out a pencil and paper and check over my list of goals. I have yet to have this method fail. As a matter of fact, I sometimes find myself leaving on a dead run because I have seen so many things that need to be done.

Being tired is not the same as being blue, but the cure is some- what the same. Relax. Get away from whatever is bugging you. Put the goal seeking machine into neutral. Take a walk. Take a nap. Take another look at your list of goals. Smile! Fate works for the worker!

Chapter 13

Make Sure You Have
Your Act Together

You may be wondering why I have waited almost to the end of this book to discuss the more personal aspects of the goal seeker's life. It's simply that if I had put this section in the First Quarter, I think you would have found it very difficult to understand in relationship to winning or losing a goal.

A real winner is a completely together person in every area of living that has a direct bearing on the quality of his or her performance.

As you read this final section, you will begin to put all of the previous pieces of the game together and gain a full picture of what it takes to fulfill the many goals you are now confident that you really desire.

Some of my suggestions, reminders and re-reminders may seem unnecessary or overly simple, but it's just those simple, so often taken-for-granted situations which trip us up as we journey through life.

How many times have you, when getting off a bus or out of a cab, heard the driver say, automatically without even looking your way, "Watch your step"? He said it mechanically, from habit, and you probably didn't really pay much attention, but this time we're entering the lion's cage, so . . . WATCH YOUR STEP!

Success Can Soon Go Stale

My first taste of success in business was also nearly my last. I was under the impression that once you were in the spotlight, you had it made. You just sat back and enjoyed the rewards of all of the lumps and bumps you took while you were paying your dues. Let me tell you, I did taste and try all of those rewards, both those that fed my ego as well as my tummy. Well let me tell you, my friends, it didn't take long before both my ego and stomach had indigestion and the spotlight began to dim and I found myself in deep, deep manure. I was a drunk that no one wanted around, I missed shows, insulted my coworkers and editors and hurt the people closest to me—my wife and children. They felt helpless, they didn't know what to do to help me.

The Lord Almighty knew what I needed and He gave it to me in spades. Attention! His Attention! I had been given more opportunity than any human being deserves because He trusted me to handle them, and I failed. I selfishly thought that I had accomplished all of this success on my own and that was a big, big mistake. The Lord is loving, but He doesn't have the greatest sense of humor when you get too big for your britches! I got so sick that I was afraid I was going to live, death would have been a pleasure! Death was not a part of His plan, however. I got the message loud and clear and I joined the greatest group in the world, Alcoholics Anonymous, where I have been a loyal and practicing member for over seven years.

I set my goal to come back up the mountain, I designed a game plan, picked my team, mended my bridges and worked my grass off. I have since written five books, two video cassettes, have a weekly syndicated radio show, am a regular on several national news shows, syndicate a newspaper column and appear in the world's largest retailer's TV commercials (Kmart). All this, by the grace of God, whom I thank several times each day. And, folks, I practice what I preach in this book every day.

Mid-Life Crisis

It never ceases to amaze me: so-called sharp business people, men and women, afraid to admit that they are middle aged or older for fear that they will be put out to pasture by a younger person. It's true that we are a youth oriented society, but it is controlled by the middle-aged. When do we reach middle age? The answer depends on whom you ask. Labor says middle age begins at forty and you are over the hill at sixty, while management selects fifty as the beginning of middle age and the age of seventy is the time to consider retirement. The so-called mid-life crisis is merely a misunderstanding of our personal goals at a time in life when many of us who have not been paying attention to the passing of time, suddenly consult the clock of life and feel that we may have missed the train, or, we are on the wrong one and are *afraid* to do something about either situation.

The goal seeker takes hundreds of trips in his lifetime and every trip is an adventure. Most are safe and enjoyable, others are dangerous and at times frightening. This is why the goal seeker in most cases is successful because he is willing to take these adventurous risks on his journey through life. Mid-life need not be a crisis, it can be yet the beginning of a whole new adventure.

You Are Never Too Old or Too Smart to Learn More

I have made several comments throughout this book regarding the need for constantly adding to your present store of knowledge. I also cautioned you not to get too lopsided in your interests, even though your goals may lie pretty much in one given area. You will find that diversified reading will broaden your imagination and improve your creative talents when it comes to game planning. I couldn't count the number of ideas I have gotten and utilized in my own games from things I have read—often from sources that seemed far removed from my goal at the time, but which fit the situation.

Reading improves the mind. It also fortifies the power of concentration. At the same time, reading helps you relax. Reading time is never wasted. Even the best programs on television can't take the place of reading because, when you read, great pictures form in your mind. With TV, the pictures are only on the screen. That is why I make it a "must" to read something—seven days a week. It can be a pamphlet, a magazine or a book, but it has to be something different from my usual interest. Second, I read at least one newspaper a day from front to back, ads and all. Yes, even the women's pages. I'm no fruit, but I read about cooking, homemaking and female problems just so I understand what the women are concerned about. After all, they do make up more than half the world's population.

Yes, you and I know of people who brag that they have never read a book of any kind since they left school. What fools!

Do You Really Know How to Recognize Confidence?

A good friend of mine gave the simplest and best definition of confidence I ever heard. He said, "Confidence is knowing what you are capable of doing and not being ashamed of it." We are our own worst enemies when it comes to getting ourselves in over our heads—into situations we have no more business being in than a bricklayer in a diamond-cutting contest. We get into these predicaments in most instances because we let our dream world creep into our rational world to the point that it blinds the rational.

When I was in the Air Force, I was allowed to handle the controls of our aircraft from time to time in flight. As a result, I had convinced myself that I could fly an airplane. I made this untrue statement several times. One day a good friend who was a pilot took me to task. We were going to be flying in a private plane. He asked if I could fly, and I replied, "Sure!"

So he said, "It's all yours. You fly us from here to our destination." The plane was standing on the ground with the engine running. He had called me on a downright lie that I had made myself believe. I didn't know my elbow from an apple cart about flying and I knew it and so did my friend. Sure, he embarrassed me, but I had it coming. He did me a favor by calling the bluff and I worked hard never to do that again. Cockiness, self-delusion or whatever you want to call it is not confidence. Confidence is knowing what you can do, not what you *think* you can do.

Later, I did learn to fly. I flew solo and did my cross country. I had to prove to my friend as well as myself that I had it in me.

Don't ever talk (or think) yourself into a corner you can't get out of, because you had no business being there in the first place. That's why it's so important to select the games you will play in carefully, to know your abilities and not be ashamed of either those abilities or their limitations.

My pilot friend even gave me a little verse to remember:

A lie . . . won't fly!

Weaned Warriors vs. Parental Interference

You may be a big boy or girl now, but parental interference can still be a problem. That interference may be wide-ranging: what kind of a job you should have, the kind of company you should work for, how far from the folks you should be living, how you raise your children, even if you should marry or not. Parents (bless 'em!) often come down hard on the matter of which church you attend, or don't attend. But when you were weaned from parental dependency, you were given the right to make your own decisions and shape your own destiny without interference from anyone as long as your plans and actions did not hurt anyone else. When you set your goals, they are set for your own benefit. And, of course, if you win, the whole family benefits, in pride if not materially.

Parents, I am sad to say, don't even have to be living to cause interference. If you keep asking yourself, "What would Dad think?" you could be inviting interference even though Dad has long since gone to his final resting place. Family ties are emotional ties. Try to avoid this kind of emotional interference in making your great decisions.

Conceit Is a Killer

The dictionary defines conceit as "having an excessively high opinion of oneself." My friend who defined confidence has this tongue-in-cheek explanation of how it blinds a person. He says conceit is "thinking that you know your own abilities and are ashamed of them." I can't add much to that. Conceit can cost you a goal and its rewards while confidence can darned near assure a win.

Be a Guide to Your Team, Not a Harness

What I am really saying is don't be a ball buster. Since you have so much more to win or lose than anyone else on your team, you can push people too far and get too deeply into their hair. It can be too easy sometimes to forget that your players have lives of their own and interests that are not yours. So, you find yourself constantly calling them to check on progress. Whose progress? Yours—not theirs. Well, you just have to get off their backs. There used to be signs on pay phones during World War II that said, "Is this call necessary?" A good question to ask yourself. Always try not to call during private times or on Sundays. If you have to call, talk to the person at the office. Emergencies are different. So are sincerely personal calls. Call too often though, and they'll call you—something else!

Don't Let the Rewards of a Winning Career Slip through Your Fingers

Professional goal seekers in great numbers have found that the only way they could enjoy all of the things they wanted out of life was to work for themselves. Maybe you're working for a company, but you're still self-employed in a sense if you're a goal seeker. I mean the guy you work hardest for is *you*.

In his book, *How To Be Rich**, the late Jean Paul Getty gave a bit of advice to the "would-be's." He reminds us that what a lot of new goal seekers forget is that they *are* self-employed and that part of their winnings are working capital and the other part is for personal comforts. All too often a man or woman will spend for the personal comforts until there is no working capital left. Thus, they can't get back into the game.

---

*Getty, J. Paul, *How To Be Rich*. New York: Playboy; 1965.

Your cash flow should be divided four ways. Take ten percent off the top as your own personal pay and invest it. The "children" (profit) of this money and its children's children become your long-term hedge. Next, pay Sam the Man, no matter whether you think it's too much or not. Take out his share. Put it aside and don't touch it, not for anything or anybody but Sam. Third, build up your working capital. Only you know when that pot is full. The rest goes for family needs and fun. Standard savings may also be taken from the surplus fund used for fun.

We talk about the times when the chips are down. Well, if you don't have any chips to go down, you're out!

You Can't Live Two Lives and Be a Real Success

A person who can't wait to go to work and get started on a new project is one to be admired at some times and pitied at other times. What makes the difference is the reason behind that enthusiasm. If it's because he finds real excitement and sincere interest in his job, if he really likes what he's doing, then you must admire him. If, on the other hand his enthusiasm is a mask for discontent, if his eagerness to get to work is really based on a desire to get away from somebody or an unpleasant situation at home, then pity is in order.

You will recall that I suggested that you look for losers and pound the weak side of the defense, and that I noted that one of the signs of a loser could be an unpleasant personal life. Well, the same goes for you. You can't be an effective and aggressive leader if your enthusiasm is not sincere. Make sure you really like what you're doing for the right reasons. Don't take work for an escape ladder when it should be a stairway to riches.

Take every step necessary to live one complete life. You can't be one character at work and another character at home. Do all you can to win admiration and avoid pity. If you don't you will get your teeth kicked in by the defense the day they learn the truth.

Is It Love or Toleration?

Love? Why should this be a subject for concern in a book covering practices for success? Why not? Anything that influences the quality of your performance as a goal seeker is of concern here and must be faced.

I have pointed out many instances where a goal seeker can take advantage of a weakness on the part of a person in the defensive line-up. I have showed you ways to take advantage of a person who may be protecting a goal you are pursuing. Unfair advantage? That's not what I said. I don't think it's unfair to profit from some other person's weakness nor would I want myself or any of my players deliberately to aggravate that weakness for selfish reasons.

Love—or the lack of it—in marriage or outside of marriage—can be the source of some of the most serious weakness in a goal seeker's game. It can defeat your opposition or it can defeat you if the shoe happens to be on your foot.

If your love affair is hopeless or near hopeless, you may want to seek counseling from a qualified expert on sex or marriage. And, once you have this advice, you must do what you must do to make everybody concerned as happy as the situation permits.

Often it will mean that love has been replaced by toleration, a dull emotional void that can lead no one to pleasant existence or allow peak performance in bed or in battle. You may just have to agree it's over.

Hey, Goal Seeker, How Is Your Love Life?

This is a word to you single seekers, those who are unmarried but not necessarily unattached. Your love life can cause problems during a goal-seeking game, too. Your reliability and proficiency may be super during those times you are dedicating yourself to your goal, but how do you rate those qualities in your social life? As I said, you can't lead two lives. The goal seeker should be at his or her best all the time. A messed-up love life can kill your concentration in the big game, and you know what some coaches say about the relationship between scoring in bed and on the field, but shame on me! That is really none of my business. It's your business.

Some younger goal seekers say they get along best with a string of casual relationships in the love department, but if you opt for a more permanent relationship that includes cohabiting (isn't that the dirtiest-sounding word you ever heard?) you had better make sure that both parties understand the primary goals of one another.

You can become as vulnerable in a budding love affair as you can in a problem marriage and the defense will make a play on a love affair sooner than they would on a marriage.

Uncle Sam Gets His Share
One Way or the Other

I have advised you to put your taxes aside as you go. That is to say, put aside that percentage based on earnings that you damned well know the governmental taxing bodies are going to take from you. In most cases, you will end up with a pleasant surplus.

Taxes are no game, so don't try making it one. Hire a certified public accountant (CPA) who has a good reputation and utilize the services of a tax attorney to guide both you and the CPA (each functions differently) to get you all of the legal breaks possible on your taxes. Stay away from schemes and systems for beating taxes. If you want to take on the whole government, you will lose. As I said, it's no game. The other side has all the players!

Let Me Think about It

As you become better known in the circles in which you choose to travel and your reputation as a winner grows, you will be constantly bombarded by the requests and offers of deal makers—some good, some bad, some worthy of your consideration and some not so worthy. I can remember in my early days that whenever anyone approached me with a proposition there always seems to be a deadline and they were under pressure for my answer. I asked a close and trusted friend and goal seeker how I might best handle this type of pressure. "Let me think about it!" was his reply. "You mean you have never had this happen to you?" I asked. "Certainly! Nearly every day. That's what I tell them, one and all. *Let me think about it*, and I do and I get back to them as soon as it is convenient and I have done my research."

Don't Be Afraid to Say NO

As you gather more and more winnings from the many goal seeking games you will play, you will find that just about everybody has some "good deal" they'd like you to invest in. Or, perhaps they have problems that only a loan from you can solve. Yes, and every charity in the world will beat on your door, not to mention those acquaintances who feel that since you have acquired so much, you would not mind sharing some of it with them.

As for investments, your CPA and tax attorney can help to guide you. When it comes to personal loans and hand-outs, you are not a bank. Charities are another matter. We all have a favorite or two, and it's usually better to give generously to some cause in which you are sincerely interested and with which you can become identified than to scatter your gifts out to everyone who asks.

In most cases, the best answer you can give is no. Surprisingly, in so many situations, your refusal will actually benefit both sides.

Always Be Proud to Be You and Others Will Be Proud to Be on Your Team

It matters not that your grandmas argued over who you looked the most like—your Mom's side or your Dad's side. As you grew older, the family tried to decide who you acted most like. That's all charming, but the important thing is that you are *you*, one of a kind. You may resemble some other person in your family or you may bear a striking resemblance to George Washington, for all I know, but you're still you and nobody else.

Your living conditions, parental influence, and social surroundings all go into molding your adult character and your ambitions, but when the job is finished *you* are the product. You and you only can decide where you want to go and what you want to accomplish, what you are willing to pay and by what standards you will set your rules.

So, be a "you" that you are proud of and you'll be a winner.

Your Children Will Learn by Your Example—Be It Good, Bad or Indifferent

I truly don't know how a child psychologist would rate me as a parent when it comes to time spent with my children. My four older children describe me as your average loud-bark, no-bite father. I am sure that I should have spent more time with them as individuals and I know I will always regret not having had more golden hours with the children. Still, I have never had any problems with my kids.

The oldest, Sue, is a Registered Nurse; second oldest, Diane, a school teacher; Patti majored in marketing; Jeff, an investment banker and Eagle Scout; and the princess, Kassie, is just approaching the starting line.

My wife, Ilene, and I have always believed that if you set an example as close as possible to what is morally right and give all the love you know how to give in the best way you know how to give it, the children will respond. In short, display a sincere concern for what happens to your children and let them know you care.

Mainly, if you show through your own example, that each person in your family is an individual entitled to be himself or herself, each will automatically want to preserve and enhance that precious individuality.

They will automatically become goal seekers.

Leave a Legacy of Accomplishments, Not Inheritance Taxes

"Damn! The way my old man and old lady are spending money, there won't be anything left for me!"

That's the way all too many people seem to think about their parents. I believe my mother and father gave me all that I was entitled to when they gave me the necessities of life during my childhood along with love, understanding and guidance to form my basic concepts of moral action.

Once you become a self-supporting individual, with the ability to accomplish your own way in life, your parents are not obligated to provide you with anything except family loyalty and continuing love. As for any legacy, that should not be a deciding factor when it comes to their comforts and enjoyments. It bothers me to no end when I hear of older persons denying themselves a trip or some special purchase because there won't be anything left for their children. My mother and father have given me so many things to remember them by that they will be a fond part of my memory for as long as I live—and gold will have no comparison.

As an aggressive, sensitive, goal-seeking accomplisher, you will leave your children and society much richer by your achievements than by any surplus funds that might be left after you pass. Live as a goal seeker and enjoy your winnings with little or no regard for what happens to those who are capable of providing for themselves. Let your accomplishment be your legacy.

Leave your children goals rather than gold. There is nothing more precious in this world.

Live to Be Remembered

It's called legendary. No, I'm not suggesting that every goal seeker will become a legend, but in your own circles, in the league in which you play, you can certainly become one. If your game plans are executed with class, your wins will be celebrated in the same manner. As a young police officer in Detroit, I had always heard the stories about two of the roughest, toughest, meanest, smartest COPs to ever wear a badge (in those days their badges carried "Constable on Patrol—thus COP) in Detroit. Ben Turpin and Chewing Tobacco Jones were their names. Both were black in a predominantly white force, and during the 1941 race riots to boot! These two officers could and did every enjoyable feat you could think of. So when I had the privilege to meet them I expected two giants. But neither was over five-feet six and not the least fearsome looking, except that Ben Turpin had a lighted cigar in his mouth, a stick of dynamite with a very short fuse in one hand, and a handful of wallpaper cleaner in the other. My vice crew and I had just come up against a very heavy steel door that was keeping us out of a very famous and nasty blind pig. Ben slapped the wallpaper cleaner against that steel door, stuck the stick of dynamite into the gooey glob, which held it like a candle, and applied the red-hot tip of his cigar to the fuse. The door soon swung open.

To this day the stories about Ben Turpin and Chewing Tobacco Jones are passed on and will be for generations to come. They lived to be remembered.

It's Not a Sin to Be Rich Unless You Aren't

Only those who *don't have* condemn those who do. I have seen these words ring true more often than not. The shoe often hurts when it's on the other foot. I can recall an incident in which a former labor organizer became a big businessman. When he was an elected union official, he was known in the industry he represented as a hard and fierce man in both negotiations and grievances. As a matter of fact, he was downright mean. Boy, did he spew out hate for the capitalists and bosses! After some years in the labor movement, he decided to leave and start a business of his own. Shortly thereafter, a union organizer showed up to sign up his employees. Our former labor crusader-turned-businessman damn near beat the guy to death, because now the shoe was on the other foot!

Another example is a former insurance salesman who felt the call and began to preach the Word. He had an excellent command of the English language and one of the best voices I have ever heard, as well as one heck of a personality, developed through his sales experience. When he first began, he would take any offer to preach, in any size church and in any neighborhood. His first churches were mostly poor and so were their few parishioners. Contributions for his services were small, but it didn't take long for him to become a popular preacher. Soon he was in demand everywhere, his fees became larger and he needed an organization to manage his engagements. He also acquired a new home, five or six cars, a cottage, a pleasure boat. He had, indeed, become an institution! I think this is terrific. I believe this preacher deserves his material success. When "The Man" gave him the signal, He didn't say, "You must live in poverty."

The clergyman I enjoy watching and listening to most is the colorful "Reverend Ike" who lets it all hang out and says it. Don't be ashamed to be rich and famous. Just remember "Who" gave you the opportunity and share the wealth.

I never make any excuses for what I have acquired from the sweat of my brow and you shouldn't either, friend goal seeker.

You Don't Have to Live in the Ghetto to Feel the Sting of Discrimination— Just Be Successful

I would never have believed it if I hadn't experienced it. I'm talking about discrimination. No, the kind of discrimination I'm referring to has nothing to do with race, religion, nationality or sex.

I was subtly discriminated against by former acquaintances after I had received some national publicity by appearing on not one but all of the national network TV shows. Parties and gatherings that my wife and I had formerly been included in were no longer open to us. No invitations came! On the few days that I would have free from tours and tapings, we would drop in on folks we'd always known and had good times with in the past—only to be made uncomfortable, to be treated as strangers. Our hosts were reluctant to talk and when we invited them to come our way, our invitations were turned down for one reason or another.

I finally asked a couple whose company I had enjoyed for years what we had done or said to deserve the cold shoulder? I asked them point blank. "Nothing," they replied, "You're just out of our class now that you are famous." That, I thought, was pure nonsense. "I'm no different than I was before," I said. "Oh, yes you are," they argued. "You can afford to eat in the best places and travel more." I finally gave up trying to persuade them they were wrong.

The next day, on a TV show with a well-known film star, I felt I would not be imposing to ask him if he had ever faced this same problem. He said, "Sure I have Jerry, and so has everybody I know in the industry. Your problem was you made a name for yourself and the others were feeling inept for no other reason than that they envied your success and didn't have the confidence in their own ability to do the same." My celebrity friend then went on to tell me that I had hit closer to home than I thought. His own brother avoided him and his family, not for something that he had done to his brother, but because the brother felt unnecessarily humiliated in the presence of such sibling success. This kind of situation can get weird to the extent that a brother or sister will even say things like, "Mother loves you more than me."

You can avoid this problem, of course, by not becoming successful. Otherwise you will be faced with it. It's so deeply ingrained in human nature, don't try to fight it. You can live with it. It's really harder on the other folk.

Never Save for a Rainy Day, Only Sunny Ones

It is ironic that, as I sit down to write, it has begun to rain. You work, work, work to accumulate enough to cover the "rainy day" that may or may not come in your lifetime: the loss of a job or your health. You tie up both time and funds that could be invested for the pleasures and enjoyment of life. If you are to succeed you must design game plans that only contain positive attitudes, aggressive moves and forward momemtum. If you are really superior in your line of work and you were to be fired tomorrow, you would have a bigger, better job in less than a week because your reputation as a go-getter will have succeeded you.

Your health, for the most part, is determined by your conscientious attention to your everyday health habits and monitoring on a semi-annual basis by your team physician.

I guess I can sum this whole thing up by telling you that I only buy life insurance, not death insurance. I own annuities that are going to pay me for the time and money I have invested, while many of my friends are betting against themselves by buying paid-up life, which means the insurance company is betting they're going to live and they are betting they are going to die. My motto is: don't ever bet against yourself.

Let It Be a Pleasure to Mature
(The New Word for "Growing Old")

I write a garden column for a national magazine, called *Mature Outlook* for those of us over fifty. It comes out every other month and is published by Allstate. I love it because with each issue I hear from dozens of readers who have an old wive's tale or two, tips to make home gardening a little easier, less expensive, and safer, or they might take exception to one of my sometimes "kooky" recommendations. I am a big user of beer (in the garden), soap, chewing tobacco, ammonia and mouthwash, not to mention Juicy Fruit gum, mothballs, and salt peter. At any rate, the three million readers have all admitted that they are over fifty and though the kinks and clinks that come with the territory don't let us do the hundred-yard dash in ten seconds flat anymore, our experience can help us make the trip down the path of life a little easier for those who follow. Don't complain about the things you didn't get to do, or about people who got more than what you thought was their fair share. Don't waste your knowledge and experience. Stay active by joining organizations and clubs that are dedicated to helping other people and society. You are a goal seeker, a goal setter, and now it is time to be a goal tender. You are the best!

Plan for Re-Energizement, Not Retirement

When I outlined this book and was sorting out the many slips of paper, napkins, old envelopes, pages from my journal and even an old handkerchief, I noticed that I had reminded myself to include a reminder to never retire, I mean hang it all up, do nothing but fish, eat, garden, read and drink. I also noticed that each of these reminders were written after the death of an old acquaintance or friend and, with two exceptions, their deaths were premature. They all went from an active physical and mentally stimulating work pattern to full stop. Within three to five years they died. No, I do not expect to live forever, but I do seriously plan to live beyond the national average longevity. Yes I have a game plan and I am actively pursuing it and will continue. That's why it is so important for you to practice goal seeking—one goal after the other, and never let total idleness be one of them. It's deadly.

A Fool and His Money are Soon Parted, to an Old Fool It Comes Quicker

I don't have to tell you not to buy the Brooklyn Bridge, because you already know from the TV commercials that Bartles and Jaymes own it. More than one goal seeker has busted his tail to accomplish what had seemed to him and many others, an unachievable goal with riches as a reward. Nowhere in his game plan had he made any plans for the investment and protection of the winning purse. The first thing he did was enter a get-rich-quicker tax shelter scheme or some other investment hoodwink and lost it all.

Don't ever let anyone else handle your rewards. Investigate before you invest anything. It does not cost you a thing to ask questions and cross check as thoroughly on this as you would any aspect of a goal. Don't lose the rewards of your efforts through ignorance, because ignorant you are not.

Keep Playing Until Time Runs Out

This is the shortest, most meaningful section: "The riders in a race do not stop short when they reach the goal. There is a little finishing canter before coming to a standstill. There is time to hear the kind voices of friends and to say to oneself, 'The work is done,' but, just as one says that, the answer comes: 'the race is over, but the work is never done while the power to work remains.' The canter that brings you to a standstill need not be only coming to rest. It cannot be, while you still live. For to live is to function. That is all there is in living."

That profound bit of wisdom was delivered in a radio broadcast by the late and great Oliver Wendell Holmes, Jr., on his ninetieth birthday.

The Older You Get the More Recognition and Credibility You May or May Not Receive

Growing older is inevitable for all of us, but it does not mean the end of our creative input to either the business and political world or to society in general. Both individually and as a group, you have an abundance of knowledge and influence, and that influence is growing every day. By the year 2020, twenty-nine percent of the total population will be over fifty-five years of age, and as they say out west, "That's a passel of power!" From a political point of view, it can be a windfall for protecting the mature population's interests and a devastatingly powerful machine to use against those in power who threaten your way of life. Thirty-eight percent of all of the voters will be over fifty-six years of age and statistics prove that more than sixty-five percent of the fifty-five-plus crowd vote. How can this benefit the goal seeker?

If you are over fifty or closing in on it, take a good look at the knowledge and talent you have acquired, and do some research to find out where, when, and how you can plug yourself in to take advantage of your skills financially, psychologically, and physically, as well as politically. If you don't, it's terrible to waste years of effort, like a gardener who plants a garden in spring, works his grass off fighting weather, weeds, disease and insects to have a hell of a super crop and then doesn't harvest it because he has more than he can eat.

While I am at it, stop referring to your over fifty years as the twilight years. One of my best friends and my personal "Greek philosopher," Lou Pappas is seventy-seven years old and has more vim, vigor and vitality, as well as goals, than men fifty years his junior.

The Lord Really Does Help Those Who Help Themselves

I am now, and have been for the last few years involved as a team member of 166 goal seeker teams. You will notice that I said I was a team member, not the quarterback. I am part of a pilot project called "Hardrock Horticulture Center," which is an associate degree program in Landscape Nursery Management and Greenhouse Management through Jackson Michigan Community College. The Hardrock Project has a student body of 166 students at all times. Their goal is to earn an associate degree, master gardener, state chemical certification, parole, and job—all at the same time!

You guessed it! The Hardrock Hawks are inmates at the Southern Michigan state penitentiary at Jackson, Michigan. This program is so successful that the student body each year wins about 300 ribbons in county-fair competition and outscores the state college students who are also taking their chemical certification.

You have never seen a goal seeker work harder than these gentlemen, which designation they are practicing to acquire! They are attentive in class, field work, research projects, homework, and study. I have been responsible for putting many a man in the slammer in my career, every one of whom deserved to be there, but my pride in being a member of any of the 332 former Hardrock Hawks teams as well as the present class and many to come is indescribable.

It Is Not a Sin to Be Physically Attractive

What does being handsome, beautiful, attractive, stunning or gorgeous have to do with attaining a goal? One hell of a lot if it prevented you from getting it.

I know a major company in which if you are not plain looking or unattractive, you don't stand a snowball's chance in July of advancing. "He's too good looking to be good," "With all that beauty, she can't have any brains," or "She's so good looking that you would never be able to get the rest of the male staff's head out of bed," are comments that I have actually listened to. Heaven forbid if these folks found out that an employee—man or woman—had had cosmetic surgery!

Well, when you become a goal seeker, your looks, no matter what they may be described as, will have no bearing on the outcome of your goal if physical appearance is not one of the requisites going in. As part of your game plan and strategy, you will find it necessary to dress for the occasion or your role.

On the subject of cosmetic surgery, I think it is absolutely terrific that the medical profession can help people become happier with themselves by changing, repairing or improving cosmetically something that a person has felt uncomfortable with. Go for it if it's what you want—that's just one more goal!

Post Game Recap

You Be Your Own Judge!

1. Have you got what it takes to be a goal seeker?

2. Can you discipline yourself to exert the physical and mental effort necessary to gain your selected goal, even when the going gets so damn tough that you think you will come apart at the seams physically and mentally?

3. Are you willing to take a down-deep and honest look at yourself and determine your good points and weak points and make a sincere effort to improve on both?

4. Are you at the point where you will take the time to list your sincere desires and the steps necessary to achieve them?

If you can answer "yes" to all four of these questions, you are ready to play! I am proud to welcome you to the Big League of Goal Setting.

Index